A JOY-FILLED Life

A JOY-FILLED LIFE

Lessons From
A Tenant Farmer's Daughter . . .

WHO BECAME A CEO

Mo Anderson

Published by Greenleaf Book Group Press
Austin, Texas
www.gbgpress.com

Distributed by Greenleaf Book Group

For ordering information or special discounts for bulk purchases, please contact Greenleaf Book Group at PO Box 91869, Austin, TX 78709, 512.891.6100.

Cataloging-in-Publication data is available.

Print ISBN: 978-1-62634-288-0

eBook ISBN: 978-1-62634-289-7

1. Self-Help / Personal Growth / Success

Part of the Tree Neutral® program, which offsets the number of trees consumed in the production and printing of this book by taking proactive steps, such as planting trees in direct proportion to the number of trees used: www.treeneutral.com

TreeNeutral

Printed in the United States of America on acid-free paper

15 16 17 18 19 20   10 9 8 7 6 5 4 3 2 1

First Edition

Dedicated in loving memory to John
and Audra Gregg, the most wonderful
parents a child could ever have.
They taught me so many of the lessons
I'm sharing with you.

Contents

Foreword

by Ravi Zacharias

Right at the outset let me say what a privilege it has been for me to know Mo Anderson. Her life, her wisdom, her tender heart for the needs of this world, and her contagious optimism have been an inspiration beyond anything I can express. So it is a delight to write a foreword to her book.

Mo has been incredibly successful. Her life story is punctuated with challenges and momentary setbacks, but also with an unshakable belief in values that are time-tested and beyond time. She recognizes that a dream career is not necessarily a precursor to happiness. Rather, it is the wisdom gained and applied over the years that brings the greatest joy. She has answered a call greater than herself.

From that depth of understanding, she encourages her readers to "follow your dream," "find your voice," "do the right thing," and "set high standards." But above all, in both poverty and success, she has found that the greatest dream of all is to know God and to know what He has intended for our lives. No matter what your belief on things transcendent, you will gain from reading this book. Whether you are in the throes of victory or in the grip of despair, this book will touch your heart where you need it most. The reason is evident right from the start. Mo's pen reaches every heart in search of a dream to accomplish much and leave this world a better place. She is a bridge builder to people, even if they come from a completely different starting point.

So find a quiet spot, get comfortable, open this book, and dive in. Preparing the soul for a joy-filled life is more important than anything else.

With a smile on my face I say, thank you, Mo, for caring to share your heart with vulnerability and courage. Your life has touched mine, and many others. This book will spread the delight.

AN INVITATION

Ames, Oklahoma, is barely a speck on the map. The tiny, remote town sits off Highway #132 about eighteen miles west of Waukomis. Where's Waukomis? Exactly! The area is mostly farmland and it was there I was born Imozelle Freda Gregg on May 12, 1937, to John and Audra Gregg. Friends called me Imo in high school. On my first day of college, someone referred to me as "Mo" and it stuck for the rest of my life.

In 1937, Oklahoma, along with the rest of the Great Plains, was still suffering the effects of the Dust Bowl, which had devastated millions of acres and sent thousands of people to the west looking for work. The country was also trying to recover from the Great Depression, which had begun in 1929. Other headlines that year included news that pilot Amelia Earhart's plane had disappeared somewhere off the coast of New Guinea during her attempt to become the first woman to fly around the world. Margaret Mitchell won the Pulitzer Prize for her novel, *Gone with the Wind*. And Adolph Hitler had named himself führer, "leader," of the German people, promising his Third Reich would last for a thousand years.

But as big as the world was becoming, my world was smaller. My dad was a tenant farmer—the land he worked belonged to someone else. He would pay the landlord a third of whatever came in from the harvested crops. It took another third of the income to seed and plant the next crops. Our family lived on whatever was left. We lived in poverty. We thrived on love. Materially we were poor, but spiritually we couldn't have been richer.

Those difficult times provided me with an amazing foundation for the rest of my life and blessed me abundantly. This book is dedicated to my parents, John and Audra, because so many of the lessons I will share with you flowed naturally from them. I hope you will be touched by them, just as I was. There is something deep and timeless about what they taught me, not just by what they said, but also by the way they lived: have a strong work ethic, live by a clear set of values, love others, live up to the promises you make, tell the truth, seek your deepest spiritual wisdom, count your blessings regardless of your current conditions, and communicate with God in prayer.

What I am eager, almost driven, to share is how my life evolved—the challenges, the doubts and defeats, as well as the successes. How is it that the little girl riding on a big tractor and walking to school in her dress made from feed sacks ends up serving as the president and CEO of one of the largest, and most respected, real estate companies in the world? How could that little girl go from dire poverty to abundant wealth? It just doesn't seem possible. But it happened.

I want to pass along the wisdom I have been given: the lessons learned by a tenant farmer's daughter. I want to share my journey with you. I want my grandchildren and future generations to know these stories, and even more importantly, the life lessons they taught me. I want anyone who reads this book to understand my perspective on what really matters in life. Having always been a teacher, I have a lesson plan to offer. It is my sincere desire that what I write will touch your heart, guide your actions, and inspire your life.

I prayerfully hope that through this sharing you will glean deeper insights into your own life's values, and that my personal stories will bring to the surface memorable ones of yours.

The stories are real; some are tough and some are touching. All of them are extremely significant to me. Their lessons have sustained me when the going was rough and propelled me forward when the opportunities appeared. However, while the book is about my life, it is not an autobiography. The stories are used to illustrate the lessons, but they are not presented chronologically and they do not tell the whole tale; I might be embarrassed if they did.

Just as this book is not an autobiography, it is also not the history of Keller Williams Realty, the company I was privileged to serve for many years. While I reflect on many of the events and lessons from my time as president and CEO, the full story will be written some day and everyone will come to understand this amazing company: where it came from, how it changed an entire industry, and why it has become a model for values-based, learning-focused businesses.

Today, as I sit here at Stonemill, my dream home near Edmond, Oklahoma, I am overwhelmed with gratitude. I sense my husband, Richard, moving around our home, and I'm filled with the deep love we have built in our fifty-seven years of marriage. What an amazing life this has been. Thank you, God.

Richard tells me, "You have to connect the dots." He says that it is the small steps we take that lead to the big leaps we make. The magic is in the little things: the daily actions you take and the relationships you make. One thing leads to another, even in the darkest hours. And, suddenly, almost magically, you are in a new place filled with new opportunities. For me, this is the miracle of life. If we live it fully, my life experience says it will reward us dearly.

> *The magic is in the little things: the daily actions you take and the relationships you make.*

It has not always been an easy life, or a successful one. It hasn't always been happy. But, I can assure you: overall, it has been a joy-filled life. I want to thank you for deciding to join me on this journey.

Lesson:

BE THANKFUL FOR
YOUR FOUNDATION

"I am filled with appreciation as I reflect upon my parents—who they were, what they did, and the lessons they taught me. I long for them to have an opportunity to see the results of their lessons in my life, as I am nearing my own final chapters."

Most of my earliest memories are centered on the farm where we lived near Drummond, Oklahoma. The farm was five miles south and one mile west of town. A turn off the highway onto a dirt road led to the long driveway up to the farm and the house where we lived. Close to the house were several out-buildings including a granary, a barn, a smokehouse, the chicken coop, and the outhouse—a "two-holer." A windmill sat by a large storage tank of water for the farm animals. The buildings were positioned in a circular fashion, with the house being nearest to the road.

Like most of western Oklahoma, the farmland was flat with a few trees scattered about. You could stand in one spot and see for miles in every direction. However, there was a row of big cedar trees that ran from the house to the main road. At the end of the row I recall a huge, beautiful lilac bush. We walked along that line of trees, wearing a path through the grass, to meet the school bus each morning because it was the shortest distance to the road.

My mother had grown up on that farm. Her father died early and her mother, my grandmother, Belle

Wilson, took over their farm while raising her brood of thirteen children; Mom was number six. Years later, Dad leased the farm. We lived in the same house where Mom was born and raised.

Above the granary was an attic full of junk and stuff grandmother had stored for years. When we weren't working, I enjoyed spending time in that attic going through all the old boxes and trunks. A tattered basketball goal hung on the side of the granary; my brother and I would practice for hours. I don't recall a lot of time spent playing as a child, but I'm sure I managed to have some moments of fun. Mom had little time to play with me, but I recall friends visiting from the neighboring farm a mile away. We would ride our horses back and forth to see each other.

My deepest, most important lessons were learned as a little girl, helping out on that farm. I understood, even as a youngster, that our livelihood depended on the crops we grew. I thought every family worked as hard as we did and probably didn't realize how poor we really were. I don't know what caused my parents to stay in Oklahoma when everyone else was packing up to leave. They would suffer many hardships, yet were determined to scratch out a living there. Perhaps it can be attributed to a stubborn will to survive. I may have inherited some of that stubbornness as well as a work ethic similar to both my mom and dad's.

My dad was raised with his other three siblings in a sod house in north Texas, but he ended up in Mountain Park, Oklahoma, where he eventually met my mom at a church youth camp. He was a man of medium height with dark hair before it turned gray.

He had a kind face and eyes that twinkled when he offered his easy smile. He wasn't a big man, but years of farm work had toned his body, while hours spent toiling in the sun left his skin rough and permanently tanned. Even as he aged, he continued to work in his garden and he exercised by walking two miles a day. Dad wore overalls unless it was Sunday; then he'd wear his suit and tie to church. I suppose most would say he was a quiet man, but he could be quite talkative with those he knew well.

Mom was a small, but stout woman. She was good looking but with stern features. I always thought there were unfulfilled dreams that kept my mother from having real joy. She loved school and was so highly intelligent she left the farm near Drummond to attend Central High School in Oklahoma City. Central offered advanced courses that would enrich her education, so she moved in with a family and worked in their home for room and board while going to school.

After meeting in southwestern Oklahoma, they were married and moved to Indiana and both enrolled at Anderson University, a Christian college. However, the Depression hit and funds for school ran out. After only a semester in Anderson, they moved back to Oklahoma to tenant farm, moving from one farm to another, just to eke out a living.

Mom stayed home to raise five children, of which I was the youngest. My brothers and sister were Felix, Faith, Leland, and Kenny. My brother Kenny passed away when he was three. My oldest brother, Felix, left for the Army during World War II. He would eventually be on the front lines under General Patton's command. Then, Leland, the brother older than me by four years, also joined the Army soon after graduation from high school.

Mom could be loving and warm, especially when one of us was sick, but could also be quick to reprimand and expected a lot from us around the farm. Unlike Dad, who was sweet and gentle with his words, Mom usually spoke very directly, with little sentiment or emotion; I think I am somewhat that way myself.

My mother often voiced regret about being unable to finish college. After marriage and children came along, she just never had another opportunity to return. She had a passion for literature and was a voracious reader and a poet at heart. After she passed away, we discovered some lovely poems she had written in high school. I read them again and again. I have some of them framed and hanging in my home.

She had been an excellent student and member of the Honor Society in high school, so she insisted we perform well in school too. She studied our report cards each term, suggesting how we could do better. I vividly recall a word of advice my mother gave me when I was entering the fourth grade, which probably set in motion the pursuit of personal goals I've maintained throughout my life.

Mom said, "This year, I want you to participate on every committee you can and then volunteer to be the chairman of those committees. I think you are good at leading and have talent in that area. If you'll keep that up through grade school into high school, when you graduate you will be miles ahead of everybody else."

I took that wisdom and encouragement to heart and implemented it at every opportunity. I eventually developed confidence in my abilities to lead and delegate. Yet, at the same time, perhaps because of our poverty, there was a lingering insecurity I couldn't seem to shake.

We didn't have much materially, but we always had food on the farm. Our cellar was full of canned vegetables from the garden: okra, green beans, carrots, beets, tomatoes. And the smokehouse had enough meat to see us through the winter months.

Mom prepared our meals over an old wood stove until the house was wired for electricity in 1948 and Dad bought her an electric one. She was an amazing cook. Her fried chicken was mouthwatering and her lemon meringue and chocolate pies were famous. She churned butter and made cheese in big crocks. Community folk looked forward to the dishes Audra Gregg would bring to church suppers. I can still taste the delicious Yorkshire pudding she made; better than the finest restaurant could offer.

Mom insisted on maintaining a clean, orderly house. She believed the family could function better in a well-organized home. I agree wholeheartedly and have always been adamant that my house stay neat with everything kept in its proper place.

She was an expert seamstress too. She made all of my clothes, mostly from feed sacks. Many people may not realize that, in those days, farm feed came in strong cotton sacks with floral designs on them. In fact, some of the most exciting moments of my childhood were accompanying my dad to the feed store where he'd let me select the sacks based on which ones would make the prettiest dresses.

I once admired a dress in a store window in Enid. "Mom, I want that dress," I said plaintively. It was an expensive dress as I recall. Mom found the same fabric and trimmings, and created a dress identical to the fancy one in the window. Mom could crochet and embroider beautifully too. She tried to teach me to sew, but it didn't come easily for me and I never took to it. Being left-handed, I just couldn't figure out which hand to use for stitching and lost interest quickly.

My dad's father died when Dad was young, so as the eldest child, he had to support the family, becoming self-reliant early on. He was reluctant to accept help from neighbors and friends in the most difficult of situations. One exception was when my brother Kenny passed away when he was 3 years old and I was just 1. He died from a serious case of strep throat; penicillin was not widely available in those days. In what was referred to as a "funeral book," Dad kept a record of those individuals who helped cover the costs of Kenny's funeral, those who attended the funeral, and those who brought in meals for the family. He made sure to send letters of thanks to all the caring neighbors and friends.

The church we attended was part of the Evangelical United Brethren denomination and was similar to the Methodist church in doctrine. During this period, the church was the main site for social community gatherings and it played a large part in our upbringing. Although Dad didn't have a leadership role at church, he was always volunteering to do repairs, paint, clean, or tend the grounds. Mom was a Sunday school teacher and made sure we were up and ready for church each Sunday morning and that we behaved once we got there.

Church folk would often make comments to me about her excellent teaching. She read challenging biblical classics like the English Book of Common Prayer and the works of the Jewish historian, Josephus. She taught Sunday school well into her 80s, until several strokes left her unable to continue.

When thinking about the relationship between Mom and Dad, it was clear they had mutual respect for each other. They were not overly affectionate but they would hug and joke with each other from time to time. These small things assured us of their love. Dad bragged on Mom's cooking nearly every meal. They talked together, mostly about issues and concerns around the farm. Then, later in the evening, they would sit together in the living room listening to favorite programs on the old Philco radio. I remember they enjoyed the Fibber McGee and Molly show, Amos 'n' Andy, and The Burns and Allen Show. Of course, listening to war news on the radio became more important after my brother was drafted. Mom, however, could not just sit and listen to the radio. She had to be busy doing something, so she would sew or crochet.

When they weren't listening to the radio, Mom and Dad would be reading. Mom would read over the upcoming Sunday school lessons and related scriptures. Dad read the newspapers, thoroughly, but most often would reach for his Bible. While he sat listening to the radio or reading, I would climb on a chair behind him and comb his hair. He would let me mess it up, give him ridiculous dos, and never seemed to mind.

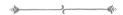

Now that I am in my late 70s, I am filled with appreciation as I reflect upon my parents—who they were, what they did, and the lessons they taught me. I long for them to have an opportunity to see the results of their lessons in my life, as I am nearing my own final chapters. When we are growing up, our parents don't always seem smart when offering guidance born from the experiences of a past generation; youth can leave us shortsighted. It is not until we are older that we see their wisdom. Today, I find myself feeling deeply grateful to have had my parents in my life for as long as I did.

In the winter of 1982, my mom was 84 years old as we gathered around her bed during her final hours. I remember my father leaning over to quietly say, "It's okay, Mama, for you to go. We won't be separated for long." Four months later, while I was planning his 90th birthday party, my dad died. For me, the closeness of their passing has always been a final confirmation of my parents' love for each other and their bond.

From these humble beginnings and based on the teachings of two wise and loving people, I grew to appreciate the hard times as well as the good. Each experience taught me things no textbook or college course could offer.

MO-MENTUM BUILDERS

- Do you know your own history?

- Record your earliest memories.

- Your foundation makes you who you are. What are your foundational values?

- Cherish your parents while they are living— it's all too soon that they are gone! Call your mom and dad.

Lesson:

FOLLOW YOUR DREAMS

"It is more than a house, it is a resting place, a safe harbor, a place of beauty and peace, a sermon in stone that moves everyone who steps inside."

My father taught me to dream. "Hon," he would say to me, "you can be anything you want to be. You just need to have a dream, work really hard, and get really, really smart. I know that once you set your mind on something, you can do it. And I will be so proud of you."

He said such things so often that, even as a child, I began to dream big dreams of who I would be and what I could do.

One of my jobs as a young girl was to walk down the country lane to the pasture and herd in the cows. While walking, my dreams first began to take shape. That worn path became the center aisle of a big church. I saw myself getting married to a handsome man and I was going to be the loveliest bride, surrounded by beautiful flowers, lots of guests, and gorgeous organ music!

Then I began to dream about what I wanted to do, what my job would be. The reality of that dream began to take shape as I developed a love for music. I saw myself being the very best music teacher ever. I dreamed of owning a black Steinway grand piano, and

I saw myself teaching little children to sing. I could picture a large audience being impressed with our spectacular performance: every child had a part, and sang it well.

My third big dream was really difficult to imagine because of the poverty in which we lived. But, with my father's encouragement, I dreamed it anyway. I could see it—my dream home. It would be a most beautiful, spectacular home with lots of rooms, and it would have indoor plumbing. As I walked that old dusty path herding the cattle, and even while sitting atop the tractor plowing the fields, I dreamed that someday I would own and live in such a home.

Would any of those dreams come true? Yes, they all did, but some took a lot longer than others.

THE DREAM OF A WEDDING

My first dream started to become reality when I was a high school sophomore and our grandmother Wilson died. The farm was sold and my family moved from Drummond to Waukomis, Oklahoma. Dad would work my uncle's land, a mile outside of town. The move was seen as a step up because our home now had an indoor bathroom. But, the real magic of this move was that it led me to my future husband.

Waukomis High School had approximately one hundred students when I enrolled as a sophomore. Among them was a handsome, standout basketball player by the name of Richard Anderson.

I met him on my first day at the school. A friend by the name of Kay Camp introduced us. Richard knew who I was, but I didn't know him at all; however, upon our first meeting he reminded me of my dad. He was quiet, a bit shy, and I liked him from the beginning. He was also tall, handsome, smart (a straight-A student), and a star basketball player on our high school team. We went to a senior play together, then dated throughout high school.

After high school graduation, I attended the Oklahoma College for Women in Chickasha, Oklahoma, now known as The University of Science and Arts of Oklahoma (USAO) while Richard attended the University of Oklahoma on a basketball scholarship. Then, for my second year in college, I transferred to the University of Oklahoma mainly to be closer to Richard. It was simply an understanding that we would one day marry and, sure enough, in the summer between our sophomore and junior years in college, the dream I imagined while walking along the pasture lane came true.

Our love for each other is complete and our marriage has fulfilled the first of my childhood dreams.

The church in Drummond was filled with people on that perfect August day in 1957. I had attended this church as a young girl and it was very important to me that our wedding ceremony be held here. The flowers, the music, and the walk down the aisle were all elements of that lovely childhood dream.

It wasn't an expensive wedding (we couldn't afford one), but it was sweet and dear to me. The entire wedding cost about $330. Two of my high school friends made my wedding dress and a neighbor made the cake for us. Because of our limited funds there was no honeymoon, just a return to jobs and school.

Richard and I just fit. The man God provided for me would walk alongside me for all these years and be my lifelong encourager. Our love for each other is complete and our marriage has fulfilled the first of my childhood dreams.

THE DREAM OF TEACHING MUSIC

I was 12 years old and we were still living in Drummond when I first asked for piano lessons. My folks scraped up the funds to pay for the lessons from "milk money" Dad made after selling milk and cream to the local dairy.

Mom so much wanted me to learn to play the piano she found a beat-up, old, upright piano that someone was giving away. The keys stuck and it sounded awful, but it was moved into the house. She somehow found enough extra money to have a tuner come out and work on the piano to make it usable. I would be in junior high before we could afford a better piano at home; it wasn't new, but it was better than the one we had. Dad paid for the piano using money from a good wheat crop that year.

There were a number of music teachers who influenced me to pursue music in my life. My first piano teacher, Bess Cozart, taught me the basic notes. She lived a mile and a quarter down the road from our farm, so I rode my pony to her house for lessons each week.

I loved to play and took to it very quickly. But, the family teased that I managed to practice my piano lessons about the same time dinner dishes were to be washed. My big sister, Faith, babied me and let me get by with it. Usually she would wash the dishes and I would dry. However, on many evenings I'd whine, "Faith, I gotta go practice."

She'd say, "Okay," then proceed to do both jobs. She was a precious big sister, almost like another mother to me. Faith died in 1992 of leukemia and I still miss her very much.

In the fourth grade, a school music teacher by the name of Nelly Brinker inspired me further. I had always enjoyed the gospel hymns at church and she intensified my interest and broadened my knowledge of other kinds of music. That year, in Mrs. Brinker's class, I started a scrapbook full of pictures of ebony baby grand pianos. I knew it would be a miracle should I ever own one, but still I dreamed.

My piano teacher saw my desire to learn and one day when I was about 14 years old, she offered, "You're talented enough that you need a really good teacher. I know a great band and choral director at the Hennessey schools, who also teaches piano. You should see if he could take you on."

Dad and I made the trip to Hennessey, Oklahoma, about fifteen miles away to meet with Earl Hanna about lessons. He agreed to add me to his roster and for the next couple of years I learned a great deal from him. I started driving (without a license) to my lessons in Hennessey when I was only 14.

As luck (or blessings) would have it, when we moved to Waukomis, I became a student of Adella Beard and Mabel Bonham. Mrs. Beard was a wonderful piano teacher who taught me to play classical pieces, including Rachmaninoff's Prelude in C-sharp minor. It was such a flashy tune that people who heard me play it thought I was better than I actually was. Mrs. Bonham was our high school choral director. She drew me more into music, fanning the flame already there. Mrs. Bonham was a master teacher who knew how to bring music to life for so many of us.

My work in music took another step forward when, at the beginning of my junior year, I injured my knee and could no longer play competitive sports. With this available time, I began to give piano lessons. Over the next two years, I worked with fifteen students of various ages. Teaching them was so enjoyable; I could share my passion for music and see them build their skills.

I also served as accompanist for the glee club, vocal ensembles, and solo performers in musical contests. I would find myself rushing from one event to another during these festivals and state music competitions. Diving into each assignment, I enjoyed helping others perform their music. I also played and sang in our school musicals. We did two major performances a year, one at Christmas and one in the spring.

As a freshman at the Oklahoma College for Women, I enrolled as a music major, knowing this would be necessary for me to become a music teacher. Dorothy Tullas, the renowned director of the college's glee club, selected me to be the accompanist for her group the following year. This was an amazing honor for a freshman.

My dream to teach music was taking shape before my eyes. I was receiving so much help and encouragement from my caring parents and teachers. They saw my passion and love for music. I absorbed music, lived it, and thrived on it. But the next year, that dream received a crushing blow.

I had transferred to Oklahoma University to be near Richard, and felt a degree from OU would carry more weight for my future aspirations. I enrolled as a music major, of course, but there was a problem. I had to work to afford school. My jobs would need to be after I had finished my daytime classes. That meant I would be working late into the evening. However, all the university music rooms closed at ten at night. Therefore, I wouldn't be able to practice. If I couldn't practice, there was no way I could complete a degree in music. I was forced to switch my major to elementary education. In my youthful naïveté and passionate pursuit of the first of my dreams—a wedding and a lifelong marriage—I did not realize that I would be sacrificing another.

I was devastated. In fact, I stopped playing music for the rest of my college career. I completed my degree, but knew it wouldn't get me the music teaching job I had dreamed of.

However, I was blessed once again. Although I believed my dream was out of reach, God saw fit to help me fulfill it. I did become a music teacher after all. In fact, I spent fourteen years teaching music, and what a joyous and satisfying journey it was. I will tell that amazing story in the next chapter.

By the way, remember that grand piano I dreamed of owning? I was 44 years old when my first ebony Steinway grand piano arrived at our home. The deliveryman thought something was wrong because I cried and cried. I was remembering the pictures of pianos I used to cut out and place in a scrapbook as a little girl, dreaming of owning such a treasure.

THE DREAM OF A GRAND HOUSE

The homes of my childhood were simple and stark. Our first house was a small farm home. I have always referred to it as "the dust bowl house." It was probably about 800 square feet with two bedrooms: parents in one and the kids shared the other. We used a wood stove for heat and Mom also cooked on it. The house was so poorly constructed rain would pour through the cracks; mice and other varmints would find their way in through the holes in the floor. Buckets were placed throughout the house to catch the rain leaking from the roof. My mother and sister told me of the time they found a snake in my bed when I was a baby. In the summer, we constantly had to shoo away all the flies with tea towels.

Then we moved to Grandmother's house on the farm near Drummond. It was an old two-story farmhouse that had seen its better days. There were three bedrooms upstairs and one down, a living room (used only on Sundays), a dining room, kitchen, and enclosed porch. The porch is where we spent hours bending over the cream separator that allowed us to produce big cans of milk and smaller cans of cream for pickup by the distributors. The north side of the house was in particularly bad shape with peeling paint and gaping holes in the frame. Dad did his best to patch the bad places again and again.

There was no electricity. Only one room (the dining room) was heated by a coal stove. I recall how happy Mom was when the home was wired for electricity. You'd have thought she had died and gone to heaven. But, we still had to use an outhouse until our move to Waukomis.

The Waukomis home was barely a step up. I remember how cold it was inside. But the bathroom, while primitive, was indoors!

After our marriage, Richard and I rented houses until 1966, when we were able to buy our first home in Ponca City, Oklahoma. I remember it cost $18,000 and we thought that was a fortune. The house had everything we wanted: three bedrooms, two baths, and a nice-sized backyard for the children. The feature that sold us on this house was a huge family room with a fireplace and hearth. I could visualize our families gathering around that big fireplace during holidays, which they did. We lived there for eight years, until January of 1974, when we sold the home for $28,000 and moved to Edmond.

We would, over time, own two houses in Edmond. The first one was a nice home with 2,100 square feet; it was a mansion to us. Later, the second house was even nicer. It was a wonderful home. Whenever my parents came to visit us, they would call it a "dream home." We would live here for more than thirty years.

It wasn't until we were both 73 that we moved into our true dream home, on May 3, 2010. We call it Stonemill. I will tell you

It is more than a house, it is a resting place, a safe harbor, a place of beauty and peace, a sermon in stone that moves everyone who steps inside.

more about the struggles we lived through to see it become a reality in a later chapter. It was all worth it. It is more than a house, it is a resting place, a safe harbor, a place of beauty and peace, a sermon in stone that moves everyone who steps inside. In the kitchen, I have many items from my childhood homes, including my mother's salt and pepper shaker collection, a butter churn I used as a child, and crocks that belonged to my mother and grandmother. The living room holds my grand piano and my collection of antique Bibles. I appreciate our beautiful landscaping with world-class pieces of sculpture. One sculpture in the front garden of our home is particularly precious to us. It is called "The Angel Group," depicting one large angel surrounded by smaller ones at her feet. I cannot look at the sculpture without thanking God for His eternal protection and "watch-care" over us.

Stonemill has hosted so many wonderful gatherings of family, friends, and colleagues. I have seen an awed and uplifted expression on the faces of those who visit here. People tell us how Stonemill touches them. It somehow changes those who pass through its doors.

It is, in every way, our "dream home."

So, did my three big dreams come true? Wow, did they ever!

I got to marry my high school sweetheart. I am still married to that handsome athlete, my dearest Richard. We have been husband and wife for over fifty-seven years. We have two children and three amazing grandchildren, whom we adore.

I got to teach music for fourteen years, creating little "masters of music" out of hundreds of children, many of whom had never felt successful at anything before.

And, this house that Richard and I have designed, built, and furnished is a spectacular estate; as beautiful and well-built as I ever imagined. And, it has indoor plumbing!

There is a poignant scripture passage that states, "Where there is no vision, the people perish." Have you seen people without a dream? They have no hope, no vision, and no purpose. They are dying slowly, perishing a bit more every day. They lead "lives of quiet desperation."

Some lose patience when their dreams are not fulfilled immediately. They drop them, bury them, and forget how their dreams once brought them so much joy. Others just don't believe dreams are supposed to come true. "They are not real, a foolish waste of time and effort," they say. These are the saddest people of all. I shudder to think what would have happened if I hadn't had my dreams to cling to.

Find your dream. If you don't have one, ask God to reveal the dream inside you. God has put dreams into the DNA of every single person.

Are you willing to connect to your dreams? Don't listen to the "dream bullies." Dream bullies are those people who never encourage you, and instead try to kill your dreams. Don't listen to them; just keep believing in your dreams. You are never too old and it's never too late to dream. Remember, I had been dreaming of my lovely home since childhood, but didn't get it until I was 73 years old. I say to you, "never, never, never give up!" And here is the most interesting truth. The dreams never end. At 77 years of age, I still have dreams. Thank you, God.

The lessons learned on that hardscrabble farm cling to me today and conjure up precious memories of my dad encouraging me to dream even though his own life was dictated solely by the need to feed his family. Time and events prevented him from pursuing bigger dreams, yet he assured me I could be anything I wanted to be if I continued "to dream, to work hard, and to get smart."

There are many lessons in this little book you are reading. But, this one underpins all others. I am passing on my father's simple words of profound wisdom: *Believe in the power of dreams.*

Dare to have those dreams. Let them unfold and grow fully, as they will. Find your own country lane where you can let your mind discover, create, and explore those important dreams.

"Thank you, Daddy, I believed!"

MO-MENTUM BUILDERS

-» God has put dreams into the DNA of every single person.

-» Find your dreams. If you don't have one, ask God to reveal the dreams inside you.

-» Be willing to connect to your dreams. Live them.

-» Don't listen to the "dream bullies." Don't let them discourage you.

-» Never, never, never give up! You are never too old and it's never too late to dream.

3

Lesson:

FIND YOUR VOICE

"We each have a voice and it's unique to us. We just have to find it. It doesn't matter when we find it. It only matters that we keep trying until we do."

After I graduated from OU, Richard still had one more year to complete his degree. We had been married for two years and our son Rick was now 1. I decided I would look for a job as an elementary school teacher, and sent résumés to a number of local schools.

I received a call from Lester Goldsborough, the principal of Traub Elementary School in Midwest City, a suburb of Oklahoma City, about fifteen miles from where we were living. I met with him, and at the end of our interview he offered me a job.

"Mo, I'd like you to teach our high-achieving fifth graders," he said, "and I want you to be the music teacher for all our second to sixth grade students." I nearly fell off my chair.

"Of course, I would love to," I said. "It has always been my dream to be a music teacher. But, you know I do not have a degree in music. Why are you offering this to me?"

"Because of your references," he answered. "They all highly recommend you as a teacher. They say you will be wonderful with the students. And, every one of them pointed out your special musical talent. They said that you were passionate in your love of music and that you would inspire students to love music too." I was thrilled about the offer, but still felt underqualified because I lacked a music degree. I put that doubt aside and enthusiastically began to do what I most wanted to do—teach music all day, every day.

We had an amazing year. I loved my students and they loved working with me. In the spring we put on a musical performance—*The Wizard of Oz*. It was amazing. Mr. Goldsborough said he never believed that elementary school students could perform at that level. "Well, Mo," he said, "I guess I made the right choice for my music teacher, didn't I?"

After Richard graduated, he got a job offer with the Conoco Oil Company and we needed to relocate to Ponca City, Oklahoma, about ninety-five miles north of Oklahoma City. I had to leave Traub Elementary and I wasn't sure if I would find another opportunity to teach music. So after we got settled in, I took a teaching job at McKinley Elementary School.

I taught for three years and then, in 1962, I took some time to be at home with our son, Rick, and our baby daughter, Karin. During that time I began to teach private piano lessons and became very involved in the Community Concert Association.

My career as a full-time music teacher was kicked into high gear in 1965. Pete Long, who was the director of music for all the public schools in the city, asked me to join his music teaching staff. When I told him I didn't have a degree in music, he said, "That's okay, Mo, I've heard what a wonderful teacher you are and you have proven your musical talent. I know you will do a great job."

The very next year, Mr. Long was approached by the director of music education at Oklahoma State University. She asked him if they could have some of their teacher candidates do their student teaching in our school system. He said yes, and told her, "You really want to have your students learn how to teach music from Mo Anderson." She observed my teaching, and then told me she was looking forward to having her students come work with me. So, there I was, a music teacher without a music teaching degree, being asked to supervise student teachers.

I realize now, it isn't always about your certification or your credentials. It's more about having the ability and passion to do something and the confidence to do it well. These qualities can be just as important, or even more important, than a professional certification, or a piece of paper saying you took some classes. Ability, passion, and confidence are what help you discover your true voice and sing your unique song for the world. I would learn this lesson again and again in my years as a teacher.

It's more about having the ability and passion to do something and the confidence to do it well.

The school for which I taught in Ponca City, Jefferson Elementary, was often referred to as the school "on the other side of the tracks." Many of the children I would be teaching came from poor, struggling families, who had no money for nice clothes or shoes, rarely had breakfast before school, and had to scrape to come up with school fees. Some of these students were bussed in from the nearby Ponca Indian reservation. I related well to these kids because I had grown up poor myself. I determined that I would not show them any signs of pity regarding their economic situations.

One of the things I wanted to do as their teacher was to provide ways for these children to feel successful and gain confidence. I wanted them to know how it felt to do something really well and be recognized for it. So, I developed my teaching strategy with that in mind.

I decided to hold them to the same high expectations I would set for any group of children. I was determined to be strict; to expect their full attention and respect in my classroom. I handled misbehavior in private and all my students knew I was serious about what I would not allow.

I developed teaching systems as I went along, discovering which ones worked best with the children. I wanted to find music they would appreciate and enjoy. However, my first objective was to help the children sing correctly. Since they would eventually be part of a larger combined choir of 125 voices, they had to master singing on pitch and in tune with the music. Many of the children had never been taught this basic musical skill. It occurred to me one day that every human being has a speaking voice and a singing voice. So, I made it my mission to help each and every student find their own singing voice.

The technique I developed had several key steps. Very simply I would first explain that we each have a speaking voice and a singing voice. The singing voice is naturally higher. So, step two, I would have them begin to speak in their singing voice. I would tell them to do it all on the same note and it didn't matter what that note was. We practiced speaking simple phrases such as, "Would you like to go to lunch?" and "How are you today?" all in one tone.

Then, step three, I would sing a note myself and ask them to match that tone in their singing voice. In step four, I would have them do the phrase in two notes. Finally, in this part of the work, I would have them do it in three or more different notes and I began to teach them the full scale of *do, re, mi, fa, so, la, ti, do.*

I called this series of exercises "finding your voice." Whenever a student matched a certain pitch or successfully completed one of the steps, the rest of us would applaud in celebration. It was a joy to see them beam with pride over this simple accomplishment. I would tell them, "Some people find their singing voice early in life, some find it later; it just doesn't matter." So there was no failure, they were just working to find their voice. And of course, they did. They got applause all along the way and that built their self-confidence.

Later, I came to understand that this approach works for everyone, and not just in music. We each have a voice and it's unique to us. We just have to find it. It doesn't matter when we find it. It only matters that we keep trying until we do. I have helped so many adults find their selling voice, their leadership voice, and their spiritual voice. When they do find it, they know. And, they have a new sense of themselves and what they can do. Just like my sweet little children in Ponca City.

I remember very well the first musical presentation of my combined choir. It was a Christmas program held in the school gymnasium, which had a stage at one end. Parents, faculty, and a few folks from the community filled the bleachers and also the chairs on the gym floor in front of the stage. It was so gratifying to see each little face trained on me as I took my place in front to direct the choir.

The children's performance was stunning. We were swarmed afterward with people praising what we had done. Some parents even had tears in their eyes; they simply did not know their children could sing that well. Those attending went out and told others how wonderful the program was. From then on, our concerts were extremely well attended, not just by parents, but extended relatives and friends. Folks from the community turned out in record numbers; even high school students came to hear these kids who were so impressive. Many came because they just couldn't believe these sounds were coming from grade school children.

I felt confident I had found my teaching voice.

Through the coming years, I would use the principles of discipline and high expectations to teach adults to "find their voice" too. My goal became more universal as my business career expanded. I was driven to help a whole company "sing its song" in order to change an entire industry. It is my lasting hope that my teaching and leadership has helped people find their own strengths, confidence, and ability to succeed. One of my greatest joys is to help others believe in themselves in order to accomplish great things—to help them find their voice and sing their own unique song.

A few years ago, I was speaking at a Keller Williams event in Houston and happened to mention how I had taught the students at Jefferson to "find their singing voice." In the audience that day was Leslie Lessert Hitt, who had joined Keller Williams only days before. She thought I looked familiar but not until I began to speak did she realize I was Mrs. Anderson, the same teacher who had taught her to sing in the Jefferson Elementary School choir. Remembering that special time and the message I was sharing touched her heart and she wept openly. I was so blessed to reconnect with that student from years ago who knew firsthand the importance of the lesson.

We all have a song to sing and a voice to sing it unlike any other. One of life's greatest blessings will be when you "find your voice" and sing your unique song proudly, out loud, with confidence and enthusiasm.

MO-MENTUM BUILDERS

- It is not about certificates or credentials; it's about having a passion to do something and do it well.

- We all have a song to sing and a voice unlike any other.

- Find your voice and encourage others to find theirs.

- Sing your unique song proudly, out loud, with confidence and enthusiasm.

- Touch the heart. Inspire excellence, effort, and passion.

Lesson:

DO THE RIGHT THING

"When you do the right thing, you can change the course of a life."

So, how did I get from teaching, a profession that I saw as a fulfillment of a dream, to selling real estate? I blame my husband Richard. One day in 1972, out of the blue, Richard announced he had signed me up for a real estate class.

"Why in the world would you do that?"

I didn't have a positive image of the real estate business or agents in general. I recalled seeing all the tiny, shabby offices in little towns. Most had old, dangling signs. It didn't seem very professional to me.

Richard continued matter-of-factly, "We are thinking of buying our first home and the class will help us make the best decision."

Well, he was lying through his teeth. Later, he came clean and explained that he knew I had the skills and the personality to be successful in sales, so he sort of "pushed me" into the field. Richard believed that I would succeed at a high level if I worked in a profession that compensated me for my effort. He knew I was no stranger to hard work.

Finally, I agreed. We took the class together, and then made a trip to the Skirvin Hotel in Oklahoma City to take the real estate licensing exam. I was so disinterested that I flew through the test with little concern. By the afternoon, I wasn't even reading the questions. *I'll never use it anyway,* I thought. I even left early because I didn't know many of the answers.

Driving home I told Richard, "Here I am a college graduate, but I probably didn't even pass that real estate exam."

Three weeks later we received the test results in the mail. Richard had a great score, but I made the lowest possible score one could make and still pass—which was a miracle in itself. We hung our licenses in the office of a local agent, but did no actual listing or selling.

In 1974, Conoco wanted to transfer Richard to Houston, Texas, but we were caring for our elderly parents and did not want to move out of state. My parents had worked so hard to provide me with special opportunities, and it was important to me to do right by them as they came to need assistance. Instead, Richard accepted a position with the University of Oklahoma Health Sciences Center and that is how we ended up in Edmond, Oklahoma. This move really marked the beginning of my real estate career. Leaving the teaching profession was incredibly painful; however, the need for more income had to take priority to balance the pay cut Richard had to accept, to pay off college debts, to help support our parents, and to provide food for our family. So, I became an agent at 37 years old, two years after taking the licensing test that I almost failed. By the way, I would later ace my broker's exam. Motivation matters.

My career as a real estate agent did not have a very good beginning. In fact, I had a very difficult time starting out. In January of 1974, I affiliated with Bob Turner Realtors in Edmond. Months went by with no success, no closings, and no money. I became so frustrated and discouraged that I decided to give up the real estate idea and enroll at the University of Central Oklahoma to get a master's degree in education.

On August 1, I had just one listing. So, I began to pray and my prayer went something like this:

"God, I'm miserable. This isn't working. Real estate can't possibly be in Your will for me. I'm not making any money; I cry every night and my family is sick of me. So here's the deal, God, I want three solid transactions by the end of August or I'm out of here!" I knew that was pretty audacious of me and not very respectful. But, I was serious. If this didn't happen, I would quit real estate and go back to the field of education.

Weeks passed with no transactions and I was giving up hope. Then, lo and behold, on August 27, my only listing finally sold: a glimmer of hope. On August 28, I met a couple who wanted to buy a house and they found one right away. Now I had two solid deals and hope was beginning to rise in my heart. However, August 29 and August 30 came and went. When August 31 arrived, I was discouraged again and mad at God. So, I did what women do when they're frustrated. I put on my blue jeans and vacuumed the house.

While I worked off my disappointment, I said, "God, how could you give me two transactions but not a third? Don't you see that time is running out?"

At 10:00 on the morning of August 31, I received a call from my office informing me that a couple wanted to look at a house. I went with them, and at the second house we saw, the magic happened. I could tell they really liked this particular home. You can always tell, because people start mentally moving in. They discussed how their furniture would look in the home and which bedrooms the children would have. I was fairly certain this was a done deal, but then I noticed the couple had stepped to the corner of the front yard and were deep in conversation.

I had a very uneasy feeling. Finally, they walked back to me and the husband said, "Mo, we'd really like to buy this house from you, but to be fair, we have to purchase it through Lillie Mae Tillman."

"Lillie Mae Tillman?"

"She's the agent we have been dealing with for two weeks. She has driven us around, bought our meals, and our children have even spilled ice cream in her car. We would feel badly if we didn't buy through Lillie Mae."

I nearly lost it on the spot. I had come so close. I returned home in tears feeling like a complete failure. I had never failed at anything in my life, so this was new emotional territory for me. It was the lowest moment in my business life.

At 7:30 that evening, my phone rang. It was the couple I'd been with earlier that day.

"Mo," they said excitedly, "we have spoken to Lillie Mae Tillman and she told us to do the right thing and purchase the home with you."

I was elated. God had blessed me with all three transactions by the end of August. But this last one came about because a woman by the name of Lillie Mae Tillman encouraged someone to "do the right thing." She could have kept the sale and the commission for herself, but instead she told them to do the deal with me.

In the next six months, I accomplished thirty-five sales transactions and, needless to say, did not go to graduate school. Instead, I teamed up with some friends to start our own local real estate company. Confidence was restored, a direction was set, and my life would be forever changed because of Lillie Mae Tillman. Who was this lady who altered my future with one simple directive? Lillie Mae was a gracious, reserved, quiet woman who walked with a cane. Most of all she was a woman full of integrity who became my hero. If she had not decided to "do the right thing," I would never have succeeded in real estate, started a company, found Keller Williams Realty, and become its CEO.

I tell this story often because it is one of the greatest lessons I ever learned. When you do the right thing, you can change the course of a life. I cannot overstate the importance of being integrity-driven in all your dealings, personal or business. You can define integrity by using the same simple words Lillie Mae spoke, words that set me on a course of business success: do the right thing.

MO-MENTUM BUILDERS

» Be integrity-driven in all your dealings, personal and business.

» Remember the definition of integrity: do the right thing.

» When you do the right thing, it changes the course of lives—yours and the lives of others.

» You may never know the positive impact you have when you live this way.

5

Lesson:

KEEP THE FAITH

"Whenever you are tested, whenever you are discouraged and doubt yourself, whenever you doubt the power of God in your life, keep the faith—in yourself, in your life, and ultimately in God."

I was raised in a Christian home by parents who prayed and read the Bible, took us to church, and lived their faith every day. Spiritual training was not just relegated to Sundays. In the Gregg household, we were taught daily the importance of honoring God in word and deed. There was a time for family devotions every day, with scriptures and Bible stories often discussed. At the close of devotions, we all got down on our knees for prayer. This spiritual foundation was the most important legacy my parents left me.

Still, like most everyone, I experienced difficult times in my life where my own faith was severely tested. While attending the University of Oklahoma, Richard and I had a professor who had a PhD in physics, a PhD in math, and a PhD in philosophy. He taught a course entitled "Religion and Science in Philosophic Perspective." We heard if you took the class, you got an automatic B. If you wrote a paper, you got an automatic A. So we both took the class for the easy credit. (Fulfilling all of your degree requirements while starting a family isn't easy.)

I admired the professor very much. Up to that point, I thought he was the smartest man I'd ever met. He used words I'd never heard, words I didn't always understand. Like many new, young college students, I thought his intelligence was a measure of his wisdom. At the beginning of one of the first class sessions, he asked, "How many of you are Christians?"

There were about eighty students in the class and nearly every one of us raised our hands in response.

"I'm here to challenge that," he said without a blink.

By the end of the course, the professor had categorically disproven the Old Testament stories I'd heard since childhood, and the New Testament's message about the birth, death, and resurrection of Christ. Because I didn't have the theological background to challenge this highly educated professor, I began to doubt all I had been previously taught. My faith was shattered and I didn't know if there was a God at all.

It still surprises some to hear this, but for a period of five years I was an agnostic. *If God existed at all,* I thought, *He certainly has nothing to do with our day-to-day lives.* I maintained that philosophy while doing my student teaching at Midwest City and even after we made the move to Ponca City.

Old habits die hard, however, and I thought it would be good to have our little son, Rick, in Sunday school, so we attended a church in Ponca City. While Rick went to his class to hear the stories about Jesus and color his lesson pictures, I sat in an adult Sunday school class. There was no real depth to the lessons at all. In fact, what I took away from it was that as long as you were good to your neighbor, it didn't matter much what you believed.

One Sunday, however, I was impressed with a single thought that hit me like a bolt of lightning and reiterated over and over in my head. *Either Jesus was who He said He was, or He was the biggest liar and imposter the world has ever known.* That thought challenged me, and I knew I had to determine for myself, once and for all, what I believed about Jesus.

The very next day, in the Monday edition of the *Ponca City News*, I saw an advertisement that read: "Is Christ real? Basic class in Christianity at the First Lutheran Church."

I called the church and asked if they had room for two more in the class. Richard and I attended the first meeting. I don't remember everything the pastor said that first night, but I do recall that he held up the Bible, and explained how it was actually two books in one. "The first book, the Old Testament, is the history of a nation that gave birth to a man called Jesus," he said. "The second book, called the New Testament, is about this man's life and its meaning."

For the first time in my life, I really understood the message of the gospel. It was so simple, yet profound. The pastor spoke of the work Jesus did for us by His death on the cross. I took notes and have them to this day. The words found lodging in my heart as if they were meant for me alone.

I had been in church most of my life, but it wasn't until I was an adult that I truly accepted Christ as my Savior. In that moment, I prayed an honest and sincere prayer, "I don't understand all of this, Lord, but I'm going to give you my life. I'm going to do my best, based on my understanding, to give you my commitment and my loyalty from this day forward."

That one decision has given my life purpose, direction, peace, and eternal hope.

My other "crisis of faith" came after we lost nearly everything in the economic downturn of the late 1980s. That was a tough period, full of discouraging days. All of our investments in oil, banking, and real estate had collapsed. We owed hundreds of thousands.

We were determined to pay back everything we owed and we were not going to declare bankruptcy. We continued to work hard. But I was deeply discouraged and wondered how it was, that after all our hard work and right living, God would allow us to be in such dire circumstances. I didn't turn away from Him, but I have to admit that my positive faith was on shaky ground.

One day, I came home exhausted and Richard had a surprise waiting.

"You have worked so hard day and night. I want you to go to the Ligonier Conference in Ft. Lauderdale, Florida."

"That's wonderful, but what is the Ligonier Conference?" I asked as he handed me a brochure about the event.

I learned that Dr. R. C. Sproul was a noted author of more than eighty books and was a well-known theologian and professor. He presented a conference every year, and it was originally held in Ligonier Valley, Pennsylvania, before being relocated to Florida.

Richard had read several of Dr. Sproul's books and had also heard some of his teaching tapes.

"We can't both afford to go, so I want you to go. It will nourish and refresh you," he said thoughtfully.

I asked my friend, Dorothy, to make the trip with me, and in a few weeks we were sitting among a crowd of four or five thousand people enjoying each and every moment of the conference.

There were wonderful speakers. And the music for the event was glorious. The National Washington Symphony performed as an orchestra, and a choir sang beautiful, timeless hymns. Richard was right: I needed this time of spiritual renewal.

On the final Saturday night of the conference, D. J. Snell, a young fresh-faced student from Harvard University, stepped to the podium to introduce the keynote speaker for the evening. I was riveted as he began.

"As a result of this speaker's willingness to come to Harvard University to debate atheism, I have come to know the Lord," the young man said. He then mentioned that the speaker had affected many young people during subsequent meetings at Harvard. Then, he said, "Ladies and gentlemen, please welcome to the podium, Ravi Zacharias."

A poised gentleman of Indian descent with white hair began to speak. I sat mesmerized; not only by what he was saying, but also by how he was speaking: using direct, sincere words bathed in love. The last few months had been full of uncertainty and disappointment. Questions about the real estate business, our financial well-being, and prospects for the future seemed to weigh heavily on me constantly. But, as the speaker continued, the Lord began to speak to me, not in an audible voice, but in words clear and unmistakable as they entered my heart.

"I am going to bless you again, and when I do, I want you to support this ministry," the voice said. It was the first and only time in my life this had happened.

I left the conference uplifted, encouraged, and blessed. Upon my return I was looking forward to sharing with Richard what I felt the Lord had told me. However, I knew how it sounded. God had inspired me to support a guy I didn't know and had never even heard of. So, I approached the subject cautiously.

"Have you ever heard of Ravi Zacharias?" I asked.

Imagine my surprise when he held up a book and said, "Yeah, I just finished reading his book, *The Shattered Visage*. I listen to him on the radio every chance I get." It was strong confirmation to me that indeed the Lord had directed us both to support that ministry. From that day to this, our relationship with this genuine, humble, yet powerful man of God has been a blessing to us in so many ways. In addition to his ministry, we give to many other worthy charities and outreach programs. I know we were meant to share God's blessings.

I deeply believe that God has blessed me for my faith in Him. His promises have been fulfilled. You will see the proof in the stories I tell in this book. Whenever you are tested, whenever you are discouraged and doubt yourself, whenever you doubt the power of

God in your life, keep the faith—in yourself, in your life, and ultimately in God. When you do, you will be blessed. I promise. It might not be right away. It wasn't for me. I still had to work hard and deal with challenges and persevere. That's just life. But, when you keep the faith, there is no real fear. There is confidence and hope. This is the promise, His promise, that you will be blessed. Keep the faith!

MO-MENTUM BUILDERS

›» Your faith and belief in God can be the framework upon which you build a worthy, loving, and fulfilling life.

›» Your faith is an important part of who you really are. Build it, believe in it, and bring it wherever you go.

›» Keep your faith. Seek it, renew it, and live it.

›» Let your faith sustain you in hard times and guide you all the time.

Lesson:

DO WHATEVER IT TAKES

"It is my experience that you get the rewards when you are willing to do whatever it takes."

There is a flip side to the previous lesson about keeping the faith. I believe that God expects us to do the necessary work and show our determination. I think He expects us to hang tough and make do, until things get better. He expects us to be self-reliant and accountable. I don't think He appreciates or rewards victim behavior or woe-is-me thinking. It is my experience that you get the rewards when you are willing to do whatever it takes.

No bones about it ... I didn't have a clue how to operate a real estate business. Yet here I was, after only a year as an agent, striking out on my own to build a real estate company, while Richard worked for the Oklahoma University Health Sciences Center. With the help of two partners, Jerry Brown and Ruth Honeycutt, we started Titan Realtors in Edmond, Oklahoma. I could never have done it alone.

When I met Ruth, she was the top agent in Edmond. I remember I asked her a question about my business and she not only took time to tell me the answer, but she also allowed me to follow her around and learn from what she did.

Jerry was an encouraging and giving person. I was a new, struggling agent lacking confidence. She was a major positive influence on me and truly helped me launch my real estate sales career. When we decided to be business partners, her upbeat attitude carried us along as we built our new company. And, she was a great recruiter. People just wanted to be with her.

I think of Jerry and Ruth when I count my blessings. We worked very hard to build our real estate company. It wasn't easy. There were a lot of other established real estate firms. Many had been in business for years. We were like David facing a bunch of Goliaths. But, all three of us were determined to make it happen. We told each other that we would do whatever it took to succeed.

We all loved the real estate business. We loved helping people obtain the benefits of home ownership, and even more, we were attracted to being a positive influence in the lives of others: the real estate professionals who joined us. We quickly built Titan Realtors to more than fifty agents. But, the work was not easy and we had to make our office uniquely attractive. We needed to provide our agents with good reasons to join us and stay. The only things I had to draw on were my teaching experience and the lessons I learned growing up on the farm. I discovered I could use those lessons to build a work environment that championed values, teamwork, and love.

As we established the company, we decided to set up a profit-sharing program, even though we were a small business. In order to actually have some profit to share, we needed to do business "on a shoestring."

In business, particularly when you are getting started, you often have to make do with limited resources. (That means money.) We watched how much we spent on office supplies. We cleaned the office ourselves, including the bathroom, until we could afford to hire someone to do it. We did whatever it took to make it work. I had faced this challenge before. I had made it through college without knowing if I could afford the next semester. We would find ways to make money and to save money so that we could make a profit at Titan Realtors.

In 1975, after one year on our own, we became part of the Century 21 franchise system and became known as Century 21 Titan Realtors. We attended a national convention that year and saw people walking across the stage, receiving awards for their accomplishments. I remember telling my partner Jerry, "We are going to go home and go to work! Next year, we are going to be up there on that stage!"

We quickly became an award-winning office and ultimately were recognized as the third-highest top-producing office in North America (out of all 7,500 Century 21 offices). These were exhilarating times, and we were achieving our great success because of our willingness to make it happen. All the while, we were creating an environment to support our agents' efforts to do the same. We created buddy teams, made sure to recognize and celebrate the agents' successes, shared motivational stories, and got them to do skits, just as I had done years before with my students. We also took time to have inspirational moments and even to offer prayers.

I knew from my teaching experience that the best learning environment happens when people are having fun. I took that concept and planned meetings that would be both meaningful and enjoyable. Over 90 percent of our agents attended every team meeting. Everyone *wanted* to be there.

We also took things seriously. We implemented standards of doing business that would propel us forward. We decided there would be no part-time agents working for our business (all of the other real estate offices had many part-timers). In our office, agents were required to attend training sessions, come to the meetings, and support each other. Gossip would not be tolerated and keeping your word was paramount. The agents that we attracted and that stayed with us understood that our values and standards were necessary for success.

I knew from my teaching experience that the best learning environment happens when people are having fun.

Because of our commitment to standards, our support of the agents, our solid profitability, and our 55 percent market share in Edmond, we were approached, within a one-year period, by eight different interested buyers. In 1986, twelve years after we launched the business, our company was purchased by Merrill-Lynch, the well-known stock brokerage company, which had added a real estate division. What they paid us was more than we expected and represented an astounding return on our original investment. This was a real "boom" for us! But we were also living in the oil patch of the United States, and Oklahoma (like the rest of the country) was on the verge of a "bust"—unbeknownst to us. Shortly after the sale of the company, the bottom fell out of the real estate market. Richard and I lost almost everything we had worked so hard to build and invest.

Nonetheless, that prestigious national corporation saw the potential and the incredible infrastructure we had built and wanted me to help them develop the Oklahoma City market. They were so impressed with the way we did business, they asked me to serve on their national training board. I began to realize that what we were doing in Edmond, Oklahoma, could actually be the model for a national real estate company.

From 1989 to 1992, things really moved fast for me. Important decisions came one after another, and each one was a crucial step in my business life. It all began in the fall of 1989 when I got a new vision for what I wanted to do—at the age of 52. I knew it would be entrepreneurial and it would be about helping people grow and succeed in business. I wanted to train and consult agents and real estate company owners. I knew that I truly loved working in the grass roots of the industry, where the real action is.

Despite our financial woes, I resigned from my corporate executive position and launched a company I named Pro Development Systems. I needed to generate clients, but I wasn't sure how to market my services. Jay Abraham, a national marketing consultant and trainer, had sent us a brochure about his upcoming three-day seminar in California. Richard decided I should attend and said he would like to go with me. It was not an easy decision to make, because it took almost all of the money in our savings account ($15,000), but Richard felt it was an investment we needed to make.

That seminar opened up a whole new world of marketing and business promotion to me, presenting ideas I had never considered before. One of the most important was how to create a unique "pay me later" program. It was a smart investment for us. It would have been easy not to make it, but once again, we were willing to do what it took.

I put Jay's wisdom to work right away, and in 1990 my Pro Development business took off. I used the "pay me later" program and met with all the real estate company owners in the area. I told them I would train their agents and they wouldn't have to pay me until their agents made them money. It was a big risk, particularly because times were hard for us. But I believed that it would pay off if I worked hard enough. The owners really liked the idea and I got a lot of enrollments.

The deal was that I would be paid 25 percent of the commission from each of the agent's first three transactions following their training with me. It worked great. In the end, I made more money than I ever could have by charging the companies up front. Then, I expanded the program to include agents from all across the state. Eventually, I also trained and consulted with managers and the owners themselves. A risky investment in a marketing program, a risky decision to train for free, and a lot of hard work helped me turn a start-up into a successful business quickly. They were risks I knew I had to take.

Pro Development Systems was cooking right along, but what happened next opened a whole new world for me. I met Gary Keller. It took a series of accidental connections for us to get together. God often works in mysterious ways.

I was training agents in Dallas for my Century 21 colleague Mike Bowman. Gene Lowell, who would later be a key leader for me in Oklahoma, rode with me to Dallas and asked to visit a new little office called Keller Williams. I met the team leader of that office who was a very sweet, enthusiastic person. She was so excited about being with Keller Williams. She tried to tell me all about it, but I didn't really get the picture.

Apparently, she called Gary Keller, the cofounder of the company, and told him he needed to talk with me. So a few days later he called and introduced himself. Well, I will tell you this: Gary is a "do whatever it takes" kind of man. He must have called me several times a week for the next three weeks. We talked about our families, our homes, and our careers. Several times, he asked me a question about the real estate industry and we talked about that. He was always fun to talk with—smart, interesting, well-spoken, and gentlemanly. Finally, he asked if he could fly to Oklahoma City and meet with me. I said, "Yes, of course, I would look forward to it."

I didn't know what Gary looked like as I waited near the jet bridge for his arriving plane. I had told him I would be wearing a blue suit with my Pro Development nametag. I was looking for a mature, older gentleman, when a very young man approached me and said, "Hi, I'm Gary Keller."

I was stunned. "Well, I'm old enough to be your mother," were the first words I spoke to him. I think he was surprised too that I was so much older. After Gary's trip to Oklahoma City, we continued to talk by phone, then a few months later he invited me to a meeting in Austin, Texas.

Money was still tight, but I activated a new credit card I had just received in the mail so that I could make the trip to Austin. The purpose was to meet with a consultant Gary had hired and to attend strategic planning sessions over a three-day period. Personally, I really wanted to win a contract to provide training for Gary's company. But, I discovered an even bigger opportunity, one that truly changed my destiny. I am so glad I found a way to be there.

During the second day, they presented the Keller Williams economic model, its profit-sharing model, and its decision-making model. When I saw the models and heard them explained, I was sure they would work. I just knew they would work. I had done many of the same things in my Edmond real estate office, just not on this scale.

I clearly understood how the Keller Williams plan would create synergy and instill the desire in others to bring more people on board.

At 5:00 p.m. I left the meeting room in Austin to phone my husband.

"Richard, are you sitting down?" I asked excitedly.

He knows by now what that means.

"I don't want to talk to Gary about a training contract. I want to open Keller Williams in Oklahoma."

I'll never forget his next question. "What are you going to do for money?"

I didn't hesitate. "The money will show up, Richard, because I was born to do this!"

So within a period of less than fifteen years, this farmer's daughter had successfully created and operated her own profitable business, sold that business for an amazing return on investment, built a respected training company, and was now on the brink of testing a new business concept. Who would have ever imagined?

At the time, I knew one thing about myself that would ensure our success. Yes, I had my faith in God and I could see that this company, Keller Williams, stood for everything I believed about how a real estate company should be run. I could feel my passion to bring this to Oklahoma and make it work. I knew I could. But, more than anything else, I knew I would do whatever it took to make it happen.

This lesson is so important. When you face tough times but keep on going; when you're discouraged and doubtful, but still show up; when you are not sure of what to do, but you give it your best anyway—you will, in the end, succeed. Just be willing to do whatever it takes.

MO-MENTUM BUILDERS

» In any venture, you have to work hard every day. Just be willing to do whatever it takes.

» There is confidence and power in knowing what it's like to "make do," to stretch every dollar, to save up for something needed ... to even clean the office and the bathroom, until you can afford to contract it out.

» Make it fun. Get people working together. The best learning environments and workplaces happen when people are having fun.

» What you master in tough times will help you soar in the good ones.

» When you keep doing what it takes, life will keep helping you get what you want.

» When people see how tenacious you are, they will want to be in business with you. They will open up opportunities for you.

Lesson:

BUILD A WORK ETHIC

"Those who achieve true freedom, independence, and success are those who earn it. They work for it. They show up every day. They get at it. They stay with it. They get things done. They build a work ethic. It is a lifelong habit."

Whenever I look back on my amazing journey to leadership and the financial independence I would eventually achieve for my family, I know that it all happened because of one basic principle ingrained in me as a child: build a strong work ethic.

Helping my family carve out a living on the farm was the hardest work I would ever do. Watching my parents struggle to earn every dollar and refuse to take handouts ingrained the importance and pride of hard work in me.

I was helping on the farm and attending to chores as far back as I can remember. From age 6, I have specific memories of working—and working hard. There was always plenty to be done. The work I did was really meant for boys, but help was in short supply back then.

I did my chores before and after school, beginning in the early morning hours and then ending well past dark. In the summer, we would keep working into the night, when the moon was bright enough to lighten the landscape. The garden always needed tending, animals had to be fed, there were cows to milk, eggs to gather, and when it was harvest time or canning time we were twice as busy. I also had to make unending trips to the windmill to pump water for the stock tank and carry buckets to the house for our use. I was happy on windy days, because the windmill would turn and add fresh water to the tank automatically and I could fill the buckets easily. But, when there was no whisper of a breeze, I had to pump and pump for water. On hot, stifling summer days, I used to wish I could dive into the tank, but we couldn't swim in the water meant for the cattle.

Doing all of my endless chores and watching my parents work so hard helped me build an amazing work ethic.

I learned to drive the farm tractor before I was 10 years old. Prior to sunrise, Dad would wake me up, then we'd eat breakfast and head out to the fields for a day of plowing. My father worked so diligently and never complained. I've never seen a more powerful work ethic to this day. His example has served me well throughout my life.

One backbreaking chore I hated was digging out the potatoes that grew along both sides of the driveway. I bet there were two acres of potatoes growing in those long fields. Dad would plow them up, and we would have to go along and pick them up in the buckets we carried. We would sell most of the potatoes and store the rest in the cellar for the winter.

As I got older, I mostly helped Dad in the fields, while Mom took care of the canning and household chores.

Mom's work was also unending. For years, she would do the family laundry by bending over an old washboard. In fact, I remember how delighted she was when she finally had a washing machine. It was one of those old ringer-type machines but she was elated. She didn't own a modern washer and dryer until she was 70 years old.

Doing all of my endless chores and watching my parents work so hard helped me build an amazing work ethic. And, that ethic and those habits would serve me for the rest of my life.

It's not just about hard physical labor. I worked to practice the piano, do my schoolwork, and get things done for the committees I served on. In college, I had to hold down jobs to earn my way through school. I worked hard on those jobs because I wanted to keep them and get good recommendations for my future jobs. And, I still had to do my schoolwork to get passing grades and graduate.

As a teacher, I worked hard and put in long hours to prepare for my classes and grade homework. Beyond that I took on extracurricular activities like our musical performances. I took those seriously and worked hard to make them successful.

When I got into real estate, even though I struggled at first to be successful, I did the work. I showed up, I learned, and I served my clients well. As a company owner, I gave everything I had to my agents, my partners, and my staff. I was involved in the community, and when I took on responsibilities, I did the work that was necessary for the projects to be successful.

It was during this time that a very shocking thing happened. It showed me how different my own beliefs were from those of so many other people. I had volunteered to be part of a local "poverty project" where we would be helping people who did not have jobs. I was intent on helping them find meaningful work where they could earn a decent living.

I met with several business owners I knew and asked if they would have some jobs that these unemployed people could interview for. Several of them agreed. As I went to the meeting, I was very excited, having lined up four or five job opportunities. I was committed to helping the people interview for those jobs and then do well when they got them.

When I enthusiastically told the chairman of the project what I had done, she became very angry at me and said, "Mo, you shouldn't have done that. Our job in this project is to help get these people government grants." I was shocked and disappointed, to say the least. I left the group and never went back. I can't stand helping people to become dependent and take handouts from others. My life is about working with people to help them be self-reliant and responsible— to work hard and be their best. I know I adopted that attitude from my parents.

Even though we had little, it was clear that Dad would not be taking government assistance, or receiving any of the government commodities being doled out during that time. He was determined to pay his own bills and take care of our needs without "asking for handouts." So, when money was needed for bills, he hired himself out doing odd jobs around town. He built a reputation in the community for his skill at laying and troweling cement. No job was too big or too small. Even when the Depression was in full force, Dad always managed to make the extra money needed to provide for the family. When we needed new pairs of shoes or school supplies, Dad would go find some job to do. My admiration for his sense of self-reliance and hard work has only risen through the years.

"Don't depend on the government for a handout," he would say. "We'll make it on our own initiative." Years later I would be thankful for the admonition. I learned early not to expect anyone to give me anything, to take care of myself, and to earn my own way.

Because of those lessons, I think it was natural for me to end up in the real estate industry. Real estate agents are really entrepreneurs. They have to find their own clients and build their own reputations. They work on commission and don't get paid until the job gets done. Believe me, if you want to make a living doing real estate, you can't just slide by. It takes a lot of time, effort, and commitment. It takes hard work. Those who work the hardest do the best.

And that may be the crux of this whole lesson. Those who work hard get the results and earn the rewards. This is not just true for real estate professionals. This is true for all businesses, for all high achievers, and for all professions. The greatest rewards, financial and personal, go to those who do the work.

I know there are those who say "work smarter, not harder." Lots of people pay a boatload of money to go to seminars on how to be successful with less work or effort. So many are looking for the secret pill or magic answer or quick-fix webinar. There are many best-selling books about "working smarter" and "working through others." I just want to point out that both of those phrases begin with the word "work."

See, underneath it all, there is a secret to success—in real estate, in music, in teaching, in farming, and every profession. It is having a work ethic. And, better yet, a strong, consistent, persistent work ethic. When I'm training others, I stress that the most positive, workable plan in the world will not work if they won't. It's like the late Zig Ziglar said: "Success is dependent on the glands ... sweat glands."

Those who achieve true freedom, independence, and success are those who earn it. They work for it. They show up every day. They get at it. They stay with it. They get things done. They build a work ethic. It is a lifelong habit. I love the quote by President Theodore Roosevelt regarding work: "Let us rather run the risk of wearing out than rusting out."

There is one final point I want to make. Work and joy go hand in hand. Hard work isn't as hard as people make it sound. Yes, it can have its challenges and stresses. Sometimes it can wear you out. But, in the end, it feels good. It builds character, strength, and tenacity. It gives you confidence, staying power, and a competitive advantage. Here's the secret: hard work is not to be avoided, it is to be embraced. It will get you where you want to go.

Ebby Halliday was one of my personal heroes. She founded her real estate company in Dallas, Texas, well over fifty years ago. It is one of the most respected and largest independent real estate companies in the country. She died at age 104 and went to work every day prior to her death. A few years ago, I had the opportunity to meet with her for lunch. How special it was for me to spend time with such a successful, powerful businesswoman.

After some wonderful conversation, I asked her, "Ebby, what is the secret of your long life?"

She said, "Mo, it's three things. I don't smoke. I don't drink. And, I don't retire."

There it is folks. Hear it from Ebby and from me. Live well, work hard, and never stop.

I don't know of many people who can outwork or outlast me—even today, at 77 years old. Give yourself that same advantage. I promise it will lead to a life of happiness and fulfillment. Build a work ethic.

MO-MENTUM BUILDERS

» Make a strong work ethic your lifelong habit.

» Listen to what my father told me: "To eat, live, and provide, one must work. Earning an honest day's wages builds character and fortitude."

» If you are not sure you have a strong work ethic, begin to build it. Set a daily and weekly schedule of doing your work. Show up on time and work the entire time. Build your endurance, like a long-distance runner.

» A strong work ethic is a competitive advantage. You will get more done when it needs to get done. You will gain the respect of those who can give you additional opportunity. You'll be the one that gets selected, rewarded, and recognized.

» Hard work is the secret. It gives you confidence and fulfillment. It gets you where you want to go.

» Listen to Ebby Halliday: don't smoke, don't drink, and don't retire.

Lesson:

ASK FOR WHAT YOU NEED

"Before asking for something, be sure you know exactly what it is you want, and most important, you have to believe it is possible to get it."

I n his Sermon on the Mount, Christ says, "Ask and it shall be given to you." As a person of faith I have embraced that invitation many times and asked God to do those things for me that I cannot do on my own. I also learned a most valuable lesson as a businesswoman through the years: you must have the confidence and the willingness to ask others for what you need, and at times, to even ask for what you want. Many times my success has been the direct result of simply asking. Many businesspeople of all types shortchange themselves by failing to ask for what they need and keep asking.

Asking has not always been easy for me. The greatest obstacle to overcome is the fear of rejection. Once you master that fear, a new world is yours for the taking. Before asking for something, be sure you know exactly what it is you want, and most important, you have to believe it is possible to get it.

I was absolutely convinced of the powerful potential for Keller Williams Realty and began to discuss with Gary Keller how I could expand his franchise concept into Oklahoma.

After returning home, I set up a meeting with eight local brokers to explain the Keller Williams model. My presentation wasn't the best, but I was very enthusiastic as I encouraged them to look at the system and consider opening new Keller Williams offices or converting their existing offices to Keller Williams. The result was less than stunning. They all leaned back, folded their arms, and one by one agreed that the system would never work.

I went home in tears. "Richard, I am the only one who likes this deal."

My husband thought for a moment, then responded. "Why don't you open an office, validate the concept, and *then* go build the region? You should call Paul Woolsey and John Bridwell."

We had been in a bank partnership with Paul and John previously. The bank was one of the casualties of the Oil Bust. All of us lost a great deal of money. As you know, Richard and I lost just about everything, while Paul and John stayed afloat due to other solid investments.

I didn't know how keen the men would be to hear an investment idea from me.

"I have something I want to show you. You don't have to do it, but you do have to listen," I told them both over the phone.

I was eager to duplicate the Keller Williams real estate model in Oklahoma, but I knew it would take funds I didn't have. I would need to be very creative to establish our first office. I needed investor partners to help finance the start-up. Asking for what I needed was so important in this moment.

But as Paul and John drove over to meet at our home on a Monday afternoon, John was adamant. "I don't care what kind of deal Mo Anderson has, I'm not doing it," he said to Paul. They were meeting with me only out of a sense of loyalty and friendship.

I was much better prepared this time as I laid out the Keller Williams model and presented the reasons I knew it would work in Oklahoma. I wasn't even halfway through when John spoke up, "How much money do you need?"

"Well, I need you to go to the bank and sign the note to borrow the money. And, I will not take a dime out of the business until that bank loan is paid off." I knew that was the right thing to do. In addition, I told them that for showing their confidence in me and providing financial support I would give them 40 percent ownership in the office.

John turned to Paul and asked, "Are you in?"

"Yes," I heard Paul say and it was music to my ears.

I reported to Gary Keller the outcome of the meeting and he was very excited for me and for the growth of Keller Williams outside of Texas.

The three of us—John, Paul, and I—launched our first Keller Williams office in northwest Oklahoma City. Paul was an excellent financial mentor. He began to study the business model and do the numbers. He would pore over information from other similar offices. Then, he would do budgeting projections and detailed financial analysis. I remember once he turned to me in a meeting and said, "Mo, do you know this model is almost recession-proof?" I was so happy that they finally understood what I had believed all along.

Of course, those first few months of doing business as Keller Williams were not easy. I knew my work had just begun. This new venture demanded my most focused efforts and skill. Within just six months, we took the daring step of opening a second office in Edmond. We knew we would need a solid group of experienced and respected agents in that area to help get it started. We called them a "Core Group" and that concept would later be adopted across the Keller Williams system.

We asked six outstanding agents to be our Core Group members and we offered them the opportunity to each buy in for a percentage of the business. Those brave folks were Carlita Walters, Dennis Nevius, Gary Atchley, Bob and Jerry Brown, and Charles Tritthart. They were excited about the new frontier we were exploring and they were up for the challenge.

So, by 1993, I was the regional director for Keller Williams Realty in Oklahoma and the co-owner of two Keller Williams market centers in the Oklahoma City area. But almost no one knew the name Keller Williams in Oklahoma. It took a pioneering spirit to open this virgin territory.

I learned to be daring and bold enough to ask. I asked agents to come to our company and I asked others to open Keller Williams offices. I asked them,

"Are you a pioneer?" I just kept asking people to join us—ask, ask, ask. Soon they did, more and more.

We were trying to accomplish something huge from a real estate business point of view. For me, there was no turning back; we would stay the course. We had a vision for what we wanted and we just kept asking for what we needed. That is what it takes; this is the commitment of a true pioneer.

Both Paul Woolsey and John Bridwell will verify that the investment they made in me, and Keller Williams, was the best they ever made— they earned a great return. It took courage and determination to ask for what I needed *I learned to be daring and bold enough to ask.* from them, but I am so happy I did. The success we accomplished over the first three-year period would be noticed by others and would lead to a once-in-a-lifetime leadership offer for me.

Asking for what you want is one of the greatest lessons I ever learned. Like the Bible says in James 4:2, "You have not, because you ask not." Be sure to ask for what you need. And, after that, go for what you want. Because, I know this from my own life: it will be given, you will receive.

MO-MENTUM BUILDERS

- » Overcome your fear of rejection. Once you master that fear, a new world is yours for the taking.

- » Know exactly what it is you most need and what you most want. Then just believe it is possible to get it.

- » Dare to be bold and ask for what you want.

- » What is needed will become clear as you move along your path. And when you know it, ask for it.

- » Remember this Biblical wisdom: "You have not, because you ask not."

Lesson:

STICK TO YOUR WORD

"One of the most important
fundamentals in business as well
as within one's personal life is
the decision to not only *make*
commitments, but to *keep* them."

There was a time, not so long ago, when one's word was as good as a signed contract, and a firm handshake sealed all deals, big or small. I watched my father do business with local merchants, landowners, and hired hands, and always there was a handshake at the end. That handshake said, "I trust you to keep your word and you can count on me to do the same."

These days, with any business agreement, there is a mound of paperwork to review and one or more lawyers present, just to make sure all parties are represented and the papers are signed correctly. I miss the old days when a handshake was the most important evidence of a done deal. I've shaken hands across a conference table or desk many times in my career. Even after paperwork is signed, the handshake is still an important part of solidifying the fact that you will honor your word or commitment.

One of the most important fundamentals in business as well as within one's personal life is the decision to not only make commitments, but to keep them. I could never imagine turning my back on a commitment because it was just too tough for me. Once a commitment is made, it is critical for you to honor that commitment.

I realized early on in teaching that it is natural for children to seek the easy way out—to avoid homework, tell a white lie, or act up to get their way. I knew they would not learn true happiness and purpose if I didn't demonstrate commitment and expect commitment from them as well.

Through the three years of establishing two Keller Williams market centers in the Oklahoma City area, I learned even more about commitment. While we were financially strapped at the beginning, I had made a commitment to my two investing partners that I wouldn't take any dividends until the bank loan was paid off. Those were difficult days, but I had made a promise, and I was honor-bound to keep it.

Interestingly, after returning from Austin, Texas, right before we launched our region and established our offices, there was another event that truly tested my resolve and whether I would keep my word. It wasn't a test of honesty or integrity, which is never in question with me. It was a test about whether I would follow through on something even when I wasn't legally required to. In truth, I was tempted.

In the fall of 1992, Dave Jenks, who I respected for the leadership he brought to the Century 21 organization, had just been promoted to divisional president of Century 21 South Central States. He was now in charge of seven states and more than 600 offices. He called and said he wanted to talk with me about an important matter. Richard and I drove south to Ardmore, where we met with Dave at a restaurant on I-35.

Dave is an articulate and persuasive leader. He indicated the respect he had for me and was very aware of what I had accomplished. He said that he wanted me to work with him in building his Century 21 division. He talked about the changes he had made and the growth he had achieved during the past four years in Texas, and that it was time to bring that kind of franchise support to the offices in Oklahoma, Kansas, and Missouri. "I can't think of anyone better than you to work with and get this job done," he said.

In the end, he offered me the position and laid out a very attractive compensation plan—a six-figure base, full expenses, and a healthy bonus package based on profitability. I would also have a staff and solid budget to work with. I knew I could get the job done and earn those bonuses. And, I trusted Dave and knew he would be a pleasure to work with.

Richard and I were still dealing with our devastating financial losses from five years before. We were deeply in debt and working very hard to pay it off. While Richard was mopping up the financial wreckage, my Pro Development training business was putting food on the table, but it wasn't generating anything close to what Dave was offering me.

In addition, the Keller Williams regional venture was entrepreneurial. It would not be paying us personally until it was operating profitably. How long that might take was not clear. It really seemed like the wisest move for us to make was to accept Dave's offer.

I told him that Richard and I would talk about it; that I'd call him the next day with my answer.

That was one of the most difficult calls I've ever made. I really wanted to work with Dave. But, when I called him, I had to tell him that I couldn't accept his generous job offer. He asked me why, and I said because I had just visited Gary Keller in Texas and agreed to buy the Oklahoma region of Keller Williams.

"Have you signed a contract yet, Mo?" he asked, "Have they given you the disclosure documents?" I told him no, that I hadn't signed anything yet.

"Well, there isn't any problem then, Mo," he replied, "In franchising nothing is final until you've signed the documents. Anyone in the business, including Keller Williams, knows that."

"Yes, I know that's true," I said, "But I shook hands with Gary Keller and my handshake is as good as any contract."

My respect for Dave was confirmed, because he simply said he understood. He didn't try to change my mind. And, he wished me well in my new venture. I was touched; I even cried. I told Richard I hoped I had made the right decision. He said, "You made the decision I knew you would, Mo. It is the right decision and the future will show you why." And it did.

Not only did things work out well for me with Keller Williams, both in Oklahoma and later when I was the company's CEO, but in 1996, I hired Dave to be our COO in Austin. As I said to him, "We were meant to work together, Dave, but I needed to be the boss." We both laughed and hugged.

When I told him that I had already shaken hands with Gary Keller and had made a commitment, I didn't know how much that one decision would be blessed. But it has reaffirmed my belief that doing what you say you'll do will serve you all through your life. There is nothing more precious in business than to be considered trustworthy.

There is nothing more precious in business than to be considered trustworthy.

There are many factors that went into those years of establishing and growing Keller Williams in Oklahoma, but there is no doubt in my mind that God honored our efforts to be honest, forthright in all dealings, and completely integrity-driven. An old saying I used to hear has become passé, but it is still so important in establishing a reputable business: "My word is my bond." From fulfilling business duties to maintaining family loyalties, one's word should be as good as the words in a contract we sign in ink. Stick to your word.

» Shake hands on it. Even after the paperwork is signed, that handshake is still an important part of solidifying the fact that you will honor your word and commitments.

» Do what you say you'll do. One of the most important fundamentals in business as well as in one's personal life is to not only make commitments, but to keep them.

» Beware of the short-term attraction of doing what is convenient or self-serving. If it violates a previous agreement, you will very likely live to regret it.

» When you keep your word, life rewards you. A reputation for honesty and fair dealing is priceless.

» Stick to your word. In fulfilling business agreements or maintaining family loyalties, one's word should be as good as the words in a contract we sign in ink.

10

Lesson:

NEVER QUIT

"I am 55 years old and for the first time in my life it is okay to be who God created me to be. This must be how a bird feels when it is first let out of a cage."

While I was developing the Keller Williams region in Oklahoma, a colleague referred me to a man by the name of Bayne Henyon who specialized in behavioral testing. I thought a connection with Bayne would help me in recruiting the right people. Bayne offered his services on the condition that I fly to his office in Charlottesville, Virginia, to go through his leadership evaluation myself and allow him to validate the tests personally. Those were difficult days, financially, and I recall struggling to find the money for airfare in order to make my way east to meet him.

The test results affirmed what I knew already. I was high on the aggressive side.

I immediately began to apologize, "I'm sorry, Bayne. I've been this way all my life."

"What do you mean, you're sorry?"

"Well, when I was a kid I always wanted to be the one to run the committee, to lead the group. My aggressive nature has embarrassed my husband more times than I can count."

Bayne walked to the white board, took a marker, and drew my profile, then turned and said, "Mo, this is the profile of a CEO."

I asked, "Is that good or bad?"

"Well, by virtue of the fact that you are heading up a region, and are actually the CEO of that region, it is very, very good. Only 5 percent of people in the world have that kind of leadership profile."

I'll never forget the feelings I had as I sat on the plane during the return trip to Oklahoma. Fresh tears sprung to my eyes as I thought, *I am 55 years old and for the first time in my life it is okay to be who God created me to be. This must be how a bird feels when it is first let out of a cage.* I had always been driven to achieve on a higher level. It was an exhilarating, affirming moment.

Later, Bayne became a consultant to Gary Keller, helping him plan the growth of Keller Williams Realty. And, approximately three years after our franchise offices opened in Oklahoma, Bayne advised Gary that it was time to hire a CEO for the company. As they talked about the search for a CEO, he told Gary, "You already have one in your company: Mo Anderson."

At a regional director's meeting, Gary pulled me aside and asked if I would be willing to throw my hat into the ring. I said, "Gary, I don't want to move to Austin." I knew the position would require a move to the company headquarters in Texas. My first grandchild had just been born, and I wanted to embrace my role as a grandmother as much as possible.

When I got home that night, I told Richard, "You will never guess what Gary Keller asked me to do."

"What?" he said.

"He asked if I would throw my hat in the ring for the CEO position."

"What did you tell him?"

"Well, I told him no, because I'm not even sure I know how to be a CEO. I haven't taken any business classes and I can't read financials. And the truth is, I don't want to leave our new grandchild and miss my opportunity to be a grandmother. I told Gary I wanted to stay in Oklahoma."

My analytical husband thought for a moment, then said, "Let's talk about this over the next three evenings."

So, the next evening we sat down and Richard began the conversation. "Gary has opened a door for you and I'm not telling you to walk through it. I'm not telling you that at all. But, I am telling you that I think you should look through the door before you shut the door."

"But Richard, I don't want to leave our new grandbaby."

In his own special way, Richard looked at me and answered, "Have you heard of airplanes? You could come home on weekends and spend time with the baby."

At that moment, all I could think of was how expensive that would be to fly home every weekend. We continued discussing the CEO possibility over the next two evenings with Richard bringing up other points to consider. In the meantime, Gary continued to call and ask if I had reconsidered.

Finally, I said to Gary, "Richard is telling me I ought to look at the opportunity."

To which Gary replied, "You should."

I decided to at least go through the interview process, but I was almost certain that I didn't have the business acumen the CEO position would require.

Gary Keller flew me to Austin to interview for the job. For eight hours he asked me questions. Among them was this question, "What would be your weakness in doing this job?"

I didn't hesitate. "Gary, I can't read a financial statement. I've had a husband who's read those for me all my life and would tell me what I needed to know. I don't know how to read them. I don't like numbers ... my mind just doesn't work that way."

Gary made his notes, then for as long as I live, I will remember his next question. "What have you done since high school or college that you are really, really proud of?"

I leaned back in the chair and said, "How much time do you have?"

For at least an hour, I rattled off to him the business start-ups, the awards, the various business honors, the civic responsibilities, and the leadership positions. At the end of our time, I said, "Okay, you've asked me questions for eight hours. Now I want to ask you questions for eight hours."

To which he responded, "I'm not going to give you eight hours, but I will fly you back soon and give you half a day to question me."

As I recall, on that return trip to the Austin office I got to ask maybe five questions before Gary began talking about his vision and didn't let up until the end of our time together. I was intrigued by the recruiting process itself and how thorough Gary was in covering every detail. In fact, it was the process itself that prompted my real interest in taking the CEO position.

I came back from the meetings with Gary and told Richard, "I haven't said no, Richard, but I think you're right. I think maybe I ought to try this. If I see that I can't do it, I'll quit and come back home."

I knew Gary had been talking to four other men about the CEO position. In the back of my mind I had decided that he would probably choose a man for the job; not a 58-year-old woman like me. Then out of the blue came the call.

"I've made my choice, Mo. Will you come?" Gary was offering me the CEO job.

I was immensely flattered, but replied, "Let me think about it one more night and I'll call you tomorrow."

It was probably one of the most difficult decisions I would make, but I called Gary Keller the following day and accepted the job. Plans were soon underway for me to relocate to Austin as the CEO for Keller Williams Realty.

I appreciate the fact that Gary Keller gave a 58-year-old woman the opportunity of a lifetime. He was open to talent from anywhere and there was no differentiation regarding age, ethnicity, gender, or religious background when seeking people for positions. The company staff was a diverse mix of people I came to respect so much.

I knew my first days in Austin would be challenging, but I didn't know how challenging. I would be without my husband, who is my best friend and confidant. Richard would eventually join me in Austin and we would establish a home there, but after cleaning up our finances that followed the Oil Bust, he had returned to the university to attend pharmacy school. He was finishing his degree, so I was totally alone— no family, no friends around for support. And, I would have the pressure of doing a job I had never done before.

I was also not prepared for the demands of corporate-level leadership. The staff was warm and friendly, but the criticism from some of the franchisees and regional owners was sometimes brutally direct. I was at the center of these discussions, because people were looking to me for answers. When I had none, or related that I was still trying to find my way, they were not happy with me. There were days I had to remind myself that I had made a commitment, and regardless of the criticism and adversity, I had to persevere, but it was far from easy.

There was no time for a slow learning curve. I had to jump in and do the best I could with on-the-job, on-the-run training. As days turned into weeks, the weeks into months, I became more convinced that I could make the company's values come alive and be an important part of its growth. Later, Gary told me it was my dogged determination to learn and overcome that kept me in the position. My dear husband encouraged me constantly, "Mo, you have to go through these things in order to get the company built, but you can do it. You're strong. You can do it!"

One of the best moves I made was hiring Dave Jenks. I had heard that he had left Century 21, so when we began to look for a chief operating officer, I thought of him. I had Gary Keller take him though our hiring process so that he could get a real understanding of Dave and the talent he would bring to our company. Gary gave him a big thumbs-up; I offered Dave the job and he enthusiastically accepted. It was a great day for both of us. We would become more than just business colleagues. Dave was a valued counselor and adviser during my transition as CEO. I will always be grateful that Dave Jenks was on my team.

My training for my leadership role started years before in grade school when I volunteered to head committees and organize them into action, just as my mother had encouraged. I always accepted the role of an implementer. I may not have had the initial idea or the big vision, but I was the one who carried it out and made it happen.

This background helped me understand how to work with Gary Keller. I needed to listen to his ideas, hear his feedback, and then give it two or three days (sometimes two or three weeks) before responding or implementing a plan. He was a visionary who thought outside the box. He would often add new ideas in midstream, and I had to be ready to go in a different direction. I adjusted and got comfortable with that. He was a role model, a master trainer, and a teacher who could always see the big picture.

When I became the CEO of this fledgling but big-vision company, I asked myself, "Do I have what it takes to stay the course, to see this through to the end?" As I went through those difficult and challenging first few months, I wondered, "Is all this pressure, stress, and heartache worth it?" There were days that I wondered if I had made a mistake. I was used to being praised, receiving accolades for a job well done. However, in Austin, my responsibilities were so visible and I was held accountable daily for every perceived failure of the company. I learned there were no excuses good enough; none were tolerated.

But there was a determination born in me as a child of the plains, and no one was going to "run me out of town." Many people quit when they are up against adversity, but it wasn't in my nature. I often felt I was in over my head. But, I would not quit. I put in the long hours and worked diligently in the face of continuous scrutiny and criticism by many people. I was just determined to do it.

Many people quit when they are up against adversity, but it wasn't in my nature.

Perhaps I hung in there because I had been in tough situations before. I had to work hard to get through college, paying my own way. I had carved out a business and grew it with nothing to offer but hard work and gritty determination. It takes true courage to get up every day and fight the battles life presents.

Something else drove me too. I knew that through my ownership in the company, I could provide financial security to my family because I believed with all my heart that Keller Williams would succeed at a high level. I never felt financially secure growing up and security for my family was a gift I could give them. I would see this through, no matter the outcome.

My answer to all of my questions and doubts can be found in the success Keller Williams would experience over my ten years of service as CEO. One well-known real estate magazine featured an article about us by Jeremy Conaway, an industry analyst and consultant. He used the analogy of a rising young tree in an old growth forest. He pointed out that this young tree, surrounded by older, higher trees (other franchise companies), was rising into the light and overtaking them. It seemed that this young company was coming out of nowhere to challenge the old forest. He wrote, "Keller Williams has the DNA of growth!"

I like to think something in my own DNA contributed to the great outcome of our efforts. Perhaps it was inherited from a father and mother who would not give up, even during the darkest days of the Depression and the Dust Bowl. I am so thankful that, just like my parents, God gave me the strength and the will to never quit!

MO-MENTUM BUILDERS

- » Remember the words of my husband Richard, "I think you should look through the door before you shut the door."

- » Before taking on any venture, ask yourself, "Will I do it? Will I see it through?"

- » Give yourself permission to be bold, to be more assertive. Or, like me, even to be on the aggressive side.

- » Do not let criticism get to you. Stay strong during adversity. Be tenacious and persevere. In the end, the critics may well become your advocates.

- » Find the determination you were born with. Let it grow. Allow it to give you confidence.

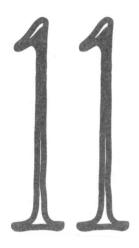

Lesson:

SET HIGH STANDARDS

"The teachers we most remember and respect are those who expected a lot from us. They set high standards and encouraged us to do better. People want to be held to a higher standard; it gives them confidence, comfort, and a sense of stability."

As I grew into my CEO position, I turned to what had made me successful in the past. I may not have had the business degree or knowledge of financials, but I knew the gifts I did possess were extremely important. You might call it homegrown pragmatism or just plain common sense. I had confidence in the abilities that had brought me this far.

As a music teacher I insisted on a student's best efforts. I taught a bunch of kids from Ponca City how to appreciate the fact that the Oklahoma City Symphony was coming to our town. There would be children from every elementary school in the area, but my kids stood out, in a good way. At a music teachers' meeting following the symphony's visit, another teacher said to me, "Mo, other kids were throwing paper wads, laughing, and acting up during the concert. Your kids sat there like little statues and behaved perfectly. How did you get them to do that?"

I was happy to explain, "I asked them to dress in the very best clothes they had. I told them they were going to a concert and a concert is a very special thing: something you dress up for. I said to them, 'Whatever you have in your closet that is the most wonderful thing you own—that is what you should wear.' Sometimes their best wasn't very much, but the point is kids behave when they're dressed up.

"Then, I threatened them with their lives if they didn't behave. I wanted them to know what a unique privilege it was. So, I made it a big deal. I let them know that I was in college before I attended a symphony concert. I wanted them to understand as fourth, fifth, and sixth graders what an opportunity they had been given.

"I also prepared them for the concert. I had them listen to the musical compositions the symphony would be playing. When they were at the concert, they knew what they were listening to and what special things I had told them to pay attention to. And, I got them excited about this special opportunity. They were riveted."

The teachers we most remember and respect are those who expected a lot from us. They set high standards and encouraged us to do better. People want to be held to a higher standard; it gives them confidence, comfort, and a sense of stability. My favorite music teacher, Mabel Bonham, would stop us as we rehearsed a number to say, "You are better than that. Let's do it again." I cried and cried when I heard she had passed away. We loved her. Mrs. Bonham was a legend. And, she impacted my life in a way she might never have known. I think we all have the opportunity to do that for others.

High expectations and high standards made me better in every area. As I worked in the real estate business, I incorporated this principle. By enforcing the high standards stated within the Keller Williams model, I determined to motivate others to be their best. I also taught them "when standards are clear, decisions are easy."

I began to implement the idea early in my work as CEO. I went to Gary Keller and said, "Gary, I need to be checking all the franchisee financials" to protect against honest mistakes, prevent misbehavior, and generally safeguard the integrity of the profit share system.

It was a practical, fundamental thing that I felt was being neglected. Guess what? We found several problems and got them corrected. We put a system in place to catch anyone who might try and take advantage of others. People knew that we were making sure that everyone was playing by the same rules.

We also created a scorecard using five numbers that had the most correlation with profitability. We tracked every market center based on those five numbers. The scorecard would show how each office was doing and how they compared with everyone else in the system. We were measuring per-

I have learned that when people are measured and compared, their performance improves.

formance (and improvement); everybody knew we were. I have learned that when people are measured and compared, their performance improves. High achievers want to raise the bar and low achievers want to get off the bottom of the list.

Sometimes office owners would complain about having their numbers made public. I knew they were embarrassed about having others see they were lower on the list. I would just tell them, "You can change that very easily. Improve the five numbers we are tracking and your office will move up the list. Then, you can celebrate and show your team how they are getting better."

Another change we implemented was to emphasize the importance of embracing and living by our written company values (I will share those with you in the very next lesson). To make these principles come alive, we posted the entire belief system on the walls of each of our offices, we shared belief stories, and we taught the Keller Williams value system at every training session.

I made it my mission to establish and enforce all our important business standards. We removed many regions and franchisees because they were not playing by the rules or living up to our documented agreements. We did it by direct communication with each owner and fair treatment across the board. Despite our tough enforcement, I am proud to say that during my years as CEO we were never taken to trial.

Here is the key to this lesson: standards matter. So, define them clearly, live by them consistently, and enforce them quickly. Even when I was operating my Century 21 office, I de-hired people who were not committed to training or hard work or our values. Once, I had to remove my top producer because she cheated on a transaction. I learned then that no transaction is worth your reputation.

Here's the often-misunderstood truth: most people are willing to do the right things; they just want to know that others are also singing off the same sheet of music. When you refuse to let some people get away with bad behavior, the rest will appreciate it.

I remember a very clear incident of that. I had told all my staff at the Keller Williams Realty International office that there was to be no drinking, no swearing, and no dirty jokes by any of the staff at any KW event. At our annual convention, one of my key staff members got drunk and was yelling, even swearing, at some of our agents and franchisees. When we got back to Austin, I de-hired her. She was defensive and then apologetic. Neither approach works with me. The standard was clear and she had violated it. There was no recourse.

High standards and high expectations go hand in hand. The first sets the foundation and the second pushes up the ceiling.

Afterward, several members of the staff came to me and thanked me for what I had done. They appreciated that I had stayed true to my word. It gave them a sense of pride about being on my team. They said it gave them more respect from our franchisees. And, several of those franchisees let me know they were aware of what I had done and appreciated it. Holding to standards matters.

It may seem as if I'm judgmental. I'm not. I respect the worth and value of every human being. I leave judgments to God. In fact, I am always moved to encourage people—to give them hope and vision. I'll say, "you are special, hon, you have so many gifts and I believe you can do so much better." I want them to become their best selves—the person that God intended them to be.

For me, personally, success came as a result of my drive more than my talents. Because I expected much of myself, I have expected much from those I could influence: students, fellow agents, partners, and the franchisees that formed Keller Williams.

High standards and high expectations go hand in hand. The first sets the foundation and the second pushes up the ceiling. People respond to them. And, they like it when those high standards are enforced— they want everyone to be held accountable. It just seems to make everything else work. With high standards, life is more exciting, more purposeful, and more fulfilling. Set high standards and live by them.

MO-MENTUM BUILDERS

⇒ Standards matter. Define them clearly, live by them consistently, and enforce them quickly and fairly.

⇒ When standards are clear, decisions are easy.

⇒ People want to be held to higher standards; it gives them confidence and comfort.

⇒ Take it upon your shoulders to protect the standards of your company, your community, and your family.

⇒ Standards and high expectations go hand in hand. They make everything else work.

12

Lesson:

BUILD THE CULTURE

"The right culture is resilient. It provides a foundation that supports us, and a place we can always return to. It sustains us, embraces us, and keeps us whole."

My vision for Keller Williams was for the company to become a family of bonded people who cared, shared, and gave at the highest level. I wanted to prove to the business world that culture defines a business.

I learned the benefits of culture from my family, from my teachers, from my church, and from the leaders I was blessed to work with. I experienced the strength that these environments provided with their values, encouragement, teamwork, and love—all elements of culture. To build culture at Keller Williams, we began with an affirmation; our most important stated value: "God and family first, then business." This simply states our belief about life's priorities.

In Keller Williams, as we gained new franchisees and associates from other companies, our culture became our most powerful magnet. We challenged people to be "builders" and "keepers" of the culture, not only to benefit the company, but also their own families and communities. Later, a Stanford University research study of Keller Williams confirmed what we knew already: our cultural model was changing the world of business and setting an example for others to follow.

The first evidence that culture was taking hold were the amazing stories of people making the right choices all across the country within our company. One story I recall was about a young associate in North Carolina who had made an offer on one of his own listings. The sellers accepted his offer and the transaction was headed to closing. But, another agent brought in a better offer on this property. Even though it was not required, he went back to his sellers and presented this new offer. He rescinded his own offer so that they could have the better deal. They respected him so much for doing this.

He told his Keller Williams team leader, "If I were with my old company, I would just tell the other agent that the house was already sold. But, I'm with Keller Williams now and the WI4C2TS calls me to a higher standard. I didn't have to do this legally, but I knew it was the *right* thing to do."

Culture is a predetermined set of values stating the way we are going to treat each other and our clients. These expectations are shared, embraced, and acted upon by everyone in the culture. At Keller Williams we have a stated belief system represented by an acronym: WI4C2TS.

It is this belief system that determines how we are going to live and treat people. It is important to have an organization's values and beliefs in writing, on permanent display, and as an active part of the conversation. Most importantly, leadership has to model the values and live them. How can others be expected to adhere to such principles if leaders don't live by them?

WI4C2TS

Win-Win or no deal

Integrity do the right thing

Commitment in all things

Communication seek first to understand

Creativity ideas before results

Customers always come first

Teamwork together everyone achieves more

Trust starts with honesty

Success results through people

We began to make time in our meetings to share stories that would inspire, encourage, or challenge everyone. I loved the stories I would hear, like the one I shared above. Our culture was such a huge factor that when most were asked why they joined Keller Williams, they said, "The culture of the company."

Another critical Keller Williams affirmation is that the real estate agent's business belongs to the agent. Each associate has their own local sphere of influence, people who know them, trust them, have done business with them, and will refer others to them. Therefore, the business belongs to the individual, not the company or the brand. Other real estate companies believe the company owns the business. This foundational principle is a key aspect of our culture that attracts some of the best businesspeople in the industry.

Culture matters in your company. It is where you will spend such a large portion of your time. It is where you will use your abilities and get so many of your personal rewards—money, success, and so much more. So, I ask you. What kind of culture do you want in your company? Don't just leave it to others. Be part of defining it, encouraging it, and creating it. When I teach culture, I share a presentation called "The 40 Key Ways to Build Culture." Many of the ideas we include are simple; some are more complicated. But, they are all important and they all add up to creating an empowering business culture for our company.

What kind of culture do you want in your company? Don't just leave it to others. Be part of defining it, encouraging it, and creating it.

I also want you to be a "builder of the culture" in your life. Culture is about who you are with—your company, your community, and, most importantly, your family. I want you to think about what kind of culture you want to promote and build in each of these areas. Ask yourself what values you want, how you want those values to be expressed, and what you can do to promote them. Then, share your thoughts and begin to work with others to make them a reality—to bring them to life. To create a culture.

This was how our great American culture was first established through our Declaration of Independence, our Constitution, and our Bill of Rights. The founding fathers understood, and were committed to, the values of "life, liberty, and the pursuit of happiness." Early in my life, I came to deeply value our American culture and I believe it has created an amazing level of caring, cooperation, and prosperity.

Personally, I felt the power of culture in my church, my local community, and of course in my family—the love, the compassion, the determination, the self-reliance, and the integrity. It wasn't perfect, of course; nothing human ever is. But, those cultural values and role models gave us all something to look up to and live by. They became part of our identity.

Richard and I have always been deeply involved in our local Edmond community, even when I was working in Austin, Texas. For instance, I have been a member of the Chamber of Commerce, the Women's Club, and several arts organizations. Why do we do this? We do it because we want to live in a loving, cooperative, law-abiding, and positive community. I promise you, this kind of community culture doesn't happen by accident. You have to make it happen with intention and effort. But, the quality of life is better for everyone when people are willing to contribute and make it happen.

Right now in our family, Richard and I help build a culture by hosting regular gatherings where we tell stories, have fun, and share our thoughts about what is important to us. We intend to build the closeness and love of the family. We want our grandchildren to know they are loved and supported—that our family is a safe and encouraging place to be. We have Grandkids

Dinner. We watch Oklahoma Thunder basketball games and OU Sooner football games. We have a special Christmas Eve gathering that has become a family tradition. We even host an annual Easter egg hunt. All our grandchildren attend and hunt for the eggs, even some of the older ones. Our family is precious to us, so we work to build a positive culture.

Here's a powerful and relevant truth: culture preserves our values and relationships even when we are tested—even when something happens that is not in step with its values. The right culture is resilient. It provides a foundation that supports us, and a place we can always return to. It sustains us, embraces us, and keeps us whole.

Think about it, write about it, and talk with others. Gather people together to discuss it. Make a list of the ways you want people to treat each other and the values you want to live by. Then, start to work on spreading that belief system and having it come to life.

You can do this when you are, or become, a leader, but you don't have to wait. Do it wherever you are in whatever position you currently have. It may, in fact, prepare you for leadership opportunities.

People approach me all the time to tell me how our values-based culture has made them a better employee, dad, mother, friend, or boss. They point to how the way we do business has impacted their home, their neighborhood, or their organization. The idea of culture carries on. You can do the same—in your company, in your community, and within your family. Build the culture.

MO-MENTUM BUILDERS

Think about the predetermined set of values you would like to have in your company, community, and family. Here are some of the values we teach to build the culture we want:

- Make decisions that are right for everyone, not just yourself.

- Be the most cooperative team member possible; always respect others.

- Help someone else, willingly and with a smile.

- Do something right without needing to be recognized for it.

- Compliment and appreciate others regularly.

- Take the high road on confrontational issues or points of difference.

- If you're having a bad attitude day, stay home.

- Speak without profanity.

- Avoid disparaging remarks about anyone.

- Commit a random act of kindness every day.

- Walk away from any transaction that compromises your principles.

- Pay your bills on time.

- Be a can-do, get-it-done person.

- Put God and your family first, then the business second.

- ∗ Understand that the high purpose of life is to give, share, and care.

- ∗ Be accountable; avoid using excuses or victim behavior.

- ∗ Understand that a business is defined by its culture.

- ∗ Culture will become the most powerful magnet to your venture.

13

Lesson:

FILL THEIR BUCKETS

"We need to be intent on filling each other's buckets not only in the workplace, but at home and everywhere in the world. You may never know how a simple word of encouragement can turn someone's life around."

My business partner Jerry Brown first introduced me to the idea of "filling buckets." The idea
was developed in the 1960s by Dr. Donald Clifton
through a children's story. Later he wrote a book for
adults with his grandson called *How Full Is Your Bucket?*
Jerry told me that when you pay a compliment or give
recognition to a person, you are filling their bucket.
When you criticize or judge them, you are emptying
their bucket. People are healthier and more vital
when their bucket is full. So I determined to make
that work in all my companies.

I remember very clearly the way we brought this
to Keller Williams. We were working to make our
company's annual convention more memorable
and fulfilling. The first change we made was to call
the meetings "Family Reunions." We wanted every
participant to feel they were part of one big, caring
family. To set the agenda, I drew heavily on my
girlhood memories of the trips made to church camp
each summer.

Those weeklong camps were amazing. I loved them.
They were packed with Bible studies and lessons
during the day and evangelistic preaching services

at night. There were also fun times—playing games, talent shows, and great music. We left camp "on fire" for God and determined to be little evangelists ourselves. We made new friends, reconnected with old friends, and had such a great time we could hardly wait for next year's camp.

So, I began to think about ways to make our conventions more like those camp meetings. My intention was that people attending would learn, have fun, and be inspired as advocates for Keller Williams.

I realized that the heart and soul of these events in my youth came from acknowledging people and showing personal gratitude. I understood that this was about "filling their buckets." So, we decided to do bucket filling at Family Reunion. We did a lot of recognition and appreciation. We gave out medallions and plaques. We put people's names and pictures up on the big screen. We made them aware that we knew what they had accomplished and that we appreciated it. And, in different ways, this spirit lives on as the event has grown to one of the largest in the industry. It created a positive energy, it reinforced successful performance, and it helped us grow the company. Saying thank you and giving recognition are powerful motivators. Bucket filling has a pragmatic value in business.

Saying thank you and giving recognition are powerful motivators. Bucket filling has a pragmatic value in business.

We were constantly and personally reinforcing our people, building recognition and appreciation into our culture. I understood that what you recognized and said thank you for would lead to more of the same good work. Rewarding the right things increases them.

I would often take a portion of time at staff meetings to say, "Let's fill some buckets today." Then we would go around the room expressing specific gratitude or appreciation to each other. Our people came to use the term and to understand that it described what happens when an encouraging word is offered to another, a special kindness is shown, or recognition is given to someone who gave an extra effort.

I also knew that we would grow faster as a company if we appreciated those staff members and associates who were helping us grow by recruiting others. Research verified that our best team leaders were recruiting five new associates a month. So, we made sure to recognize these top-recruiting leaders. And every month we sent out thank-you letters to all those who had sponsored people into the company. We also sent letters to the agents who had just joined us, letting them know how happy and honored we were to have them with Keller Williams. I believe it truly spurred our growth.

I return to my teaching experience again and again to remind myself how important it is to praise those who are giving their best. I learned firsthand as a teacher how the simplest words of recognition would lift hearts, convince others they could achieve more, and even change their lives. Just as the students would take time to praise a fellow student who just learned to sing, it became paramount to me that as the company grew we would not forget the importance of celebrating each other's achievements, however small or large. I made sure this enriching and uplifting practice was ingrained into our company culture.

As a teacher, I also learned the difference between touching the mind and touching the heart. The kids would become quiet and listen intently whenever I shared something inspirational. It was astounding. I knew the story was touching their hearts. I could ask them to do amazing things, like sing beautifully, when their hearts were touched. Now, when I'm speaking to groups, from just a few people to several thousand, I remember how important it is to "touch the heart." So, I share stories that have touched me, motivated me, and raised my level of awareness. Only through touching the heart can one inspire excellence, effort, and passion in others.

With that idea in mind, I started a special breakfast gathering at our annual Family Reunion for all those who wanted to attend—it was a bonus session. First, we called it the "President's Prayer Breakfast," because I was the president (and CEO) and I wanted people to come together in prayer. Later, we renamed it the "Inspirational Breakfast." It soon became one of the best-attended and most heartwarming highlights of Family Reunion. Our hope was that everyone would leave the convention fired up about the company and its big heart.

As part of the Inspirational Breakfast, we gave the Bob Carter award to those who went above and beyond in their contribution to others in the company. They might be a role model of courage and faith, or they may have had a special influence on the company culture. This award is named after a very special gentleman who served as our director of technology. In fact, he wrote the initial software program and designed the computer system that tracked, calculated, and distributed our KW profit share.

One day Bob came to my office in Austin to inform me the doctors had told him he had only three months to live. He had been diagnosed with recurring melanoma cancer. I told my valued friend and colleague, "Bob, don't receive a death sentence from a doctor. God alone knows when He wants to take you home, so just put aside the death sentence." I took Bob's hand and prayed with him. Along with healing, I asked God to reveal Himself in such a way that Bob would have peace during this difficult time.

Bob lived six months longer before he went to heaven, receiving his ultimate healing. But during that time, even though he was weakened by his radiation and chemo treatments, he worked to document all of the complicated software he had built for the company and its profit share system. To me, he was a hero. He was so well loved and respected by everyone that we named one of our highest awards after him. It is given annually to an individual in Keller Williams who inspires us with their courage and contribution, just as Bob did.

So, at every level, I was intent upon our saying thank you to others for what they had done.

We need to be intent on filling each other's buckets not only in the workplace, but at home and everywhere in the world. You may never know how a simple word of encouragement can turn someone's life around.

Small acknowledgments from others like "you did a good job" or "we appreciate you so much" helped me get through some tough days. Don't withhold the words that may help, heal, or encourage someone.

I rely on my own intuition, and more importantly the Holy Spirit, when determining how to help those I care about. Sometimes I just let people in pain know I love them and that I am praying for them. I will pray for others anytime and anywhere. Prayer is the greatest power in the universe. Each day in my quiet time I ask God to direct me or impress me with someone for whom I could be a blessing. Someone may come to mind I haven't thought of in years or it could be someone in my own family.

It is extremely important to show care and gratitude in a world becoming increasingly self-promoting and full of an entitlement attitude. In the Keller Williams business model, we teach people to succeed through others. You get what you want when you fill buckets and help others get what they want. Bucket filling equals joy giving. I encourage you to do this in your life, wherever you are and whenever you can.

Fill someone's bucket. It will make their day. And YOURS!

MO-MENTUM BUILDERS

- ⟫ Remember that "bucket filling" is the term to describe when an encouraging word is offered to another, a special kindness or support is shown, or recognition is given to those who have demonstrated extra effort.

- ⟫ Become a filler of buckets. Recognize, encourage, and give appreciation to others.

- ⟫ Do it every day and everywhere.

- ⟫ Ask yourself this question: "Whose bucket can I fill today?"

- ⟫ Be intent on filling each other's buckets not only in the workplace, but at home and everywhere in the world.

- ⟫ It is even more important to show gratitude in a world that is becoming increasingly self-promoting and full of an entitlement attitude.

14

Lesson:

BE A TOUGH LOVE LEADER

"In the day-to-day handling of problems or disputes, sooner is better than later. Problems left to fester get worse with time. Issues must be attacked head on and quickly."

I was a tough teacher who didn't put up with anyone disrupting my classroom. I quickly marched troublemakers into the hall and let them know what I expected. I held their little shoulders firmly between my hands and looked them right in the eye and said, "What you did is not acceptable in my room. We have high standards and that behavior will not be tolerated. Now I'm going to expect you to go back in that room and behave. And if you don't, I'm calling your parents."

One of the reasons I had extremely well-behaved classes is that I dealt with problems immediately. I set the rules and learned early if you delay discipline, behavior only gets worse. In the day-to-day handling of problems or disputes, sooner is better than later. Problems left to fester get worse with time. Issues must be attacked head on and quickly.

I applied these disciplinary principles in every position I held throughout my teaching and business career. I knew that adults, as well as children, need boundaries. They feel secure when they know the rules. Handling conflict just comes with the job if you are in leadership, because people are going to push those boundaries. Whenever there was a conflict, I was on it like a speed demon. I would bring the individual or the two or three people having issues into my office and we would work on each issue until it was resolved.

Tough conversations are never easy. I tried to start with the positive things I knew about the person, and then move to the problem area. I let them know that I would give them three strikes and this was only strike one. By strike two, if the problem continued, I demanded resolution. On strike three, I would ask the person to gather their things and leave.

I made sure that my words were bathed in love. I always wanted the best for those I had to correct. I learned to use a special method. I called it the "tough love sandwich"—love on top, tough in the middle, and then more love on the bottom. Love-tough-love. I knew I had to be tough, but I wanted it surrounded with love. It doesn't make it easier, but it does make it feel better. And, I think it increases the likelihood that it will lead to a real change in attitude and behavior.

For example, if I knew there was a problem with gossip in an office, I would pull the person (gossiper) into my office and explain my disappointment by stating, "You know what? You're a person that I'm just so proud of, and I want you to work on this because you need to rise above it. Honey, you are gossiping. You know it and I know it. As you grow in life I want to help you overcome that. Now, let's talk about how you can discipline yourself not to do that. What do you do when you feel the temptation to talk about someone? Let's figure out some actions or decisions you can make to remedy that. Because, when you overcome this you are going to move your whole life to the next level. Isn't that exciting?"

I often tried to interject some personal imperfection in order to make them feel more comfortable and honest about their infraction. I never pretended to be perfect myself.

Here's the bottom line. Some received it well, others did not. Some were immediately offended, or defensive and combative. That is when the conversation changed to "the three strikes and you're out" policy. Especially if I had talked to someone more than once about the same issue, I would say, "This is strike one, hon. I am not going to tolerate this behavior. I'm documenting your file and now it is three strikes and you're out." I love the three strikes option because it gives everyone an opportunity to change, and if they don't, they actually make the decision for you.

Once, an employee who was facing the consequences of her third strike said to me, "I think you are being unfair."

"I'm sorry that you believe I'm not being fair, but this is my decision and you will be out this afternoon at 4:00."

"No," she protested, "you are being unfair, Mo."

I saw her later at an event and she still didn't get it. She approached me and said, "I've thought a lot since I left Keller Williams about what soured our relationship and I believe too many people came between us."

To which I replied, "Hon, people didn't come between us—it was you being naughty."

One of our most popular and successful leaders was undermining the organization and threatening to leave our system to duplicate the Keller Williams model in a franchise of his own. We learned of the scheme and I had to make the call to confront him with what we had discovered. I prayed, in my mind, throughout the entire conversation.

"Do you know what a football coach does when the quarterback drops the ball too many times?" I asked to ease into the discussion.

"Well, he puts the QB on the bench," he answered simply.

I replied, "Well, that's what I'm going to do with you. Effective today, you are on the bench. You are no longer approved to be a leader in this company and here are the reasons why."

I rattled off the list of infractions then continued. "Here's the deal. If you get these things corrected and I am convinced you are sorry for what you've done, I might consider putting you back on the field."

He became irate and I knew it was only a matter of time before the next call would be made. Sure enough, a month later I had to call again.

"I am really sorry, but I am taking you off the team. Take your market center, all your people, and go have a happy life. You are not with Keller Williams anymore."

He became angry and replied, "Well, I'm coming to the convention."

"No, no you're not," I answered calmly. "I'm refunding your registration fees and you will not show up at the convention because security will remove you if you do."

Other company leaders reported, "Mo Anderson is something else. She's got more courage than anybody I've ever met. You should have seen the way she handled it. She was so good." I had been deeply worried about what the leadership in our company's regions would think about my decision and I was thrilled to receive such strong support for doing the right thing and maintaining my tough love approach.

I am also a strong advocate of finding more suitable positions for those who may have failed at one thing but have demonstrated a great work ethic and are loyal employees. It hurts me personally to see people not succeeding. I want to give them hope, but I must tell them the truth as well. I have lovingly said to people, "You are not succeeding in this role, but let's see if there is something else you are more gifted to do."

Tough love is about demanding the best of people, but it also requires genuine care and respect. Keller Williams was once facing a possible lawsuit from one of our franchise owners over some mishandled procedures. I went to meet with him and his attorney. As I waited in a side office, his attorney (from this very big law firm where our meeting was being held) came in, stood over me, pointed his finger in my face, and said, "We are

> *Tough love is about demanding the best of people, but it also requires genuine care and respect.*

going to take Keller Williams down. Your company is going under!"

Inside I was shaking, scared to death, but I just sat there and prayed, "Lord, how do I respond?"

I decided to smile politely and say nothing.

We entered the meeting room and soon the Keller Williams owner walked in—he was the man who was threatening to sue us. Instead of going directly to his seat next to his bully attorney, he came around to where I was seated and gave me a hug. You could tell that agitated his attorney.

When all were seated, I said, "I'm the one who called this meeting, so I will be facilitating it."

I looked at the Keller Williams owner and said, "What do you want?"

He didn't blink, "$750,000."

Neither did I, "Hon, you're not going to get it. Now, let's get real."

When the owner offered to lower the amount to $600,000, his attorney stood up, pounded the table, and said to his client, "There will be no more of that. You are not to speak to her directly."

I very calmly turned to the owner and said, "Come and meet with me in the other room for just a minute."

The attorney bristled, "Don't you go!"

I acted as if I hadn't heard him. "Come on, let's talk."

Once inside the other office, I said, "I cannot stand your attorney another minute. I want us to go to your real estate office and sit down and work this out together. I do not want him present. If he comes with you, I'm headed back to Austin."

The owner was willing to do that. Between the two of us, we quickly and respectfully reached a fair and equitable agreement.

Sometime later, I became aware that others were often referring to me as "the velvet hammer." I liked that. It indicated I could be tough, but also caring and respectful. It is my reliance on God that gives me wisdom and courage to deal with these difficult situations.

Tough love comes into play in dealing with everyday issues that most companies face; however, there are some moral lapses that just cannot be tolerated. For instance, a loan originator wrote me once to tell me that one of our owners was sending her offensive attachments with his emails.

Her note said, "Mo, I hear you are a godly woman. I am having trouble with one of your owners. Would you please help me?"

She forwarded the offensive attachments to me and I was appalled at the images. You could hear my reaction all the way down the hall, I'm sure.

We called the man to a meeting in Austin and confronted him. We also had an earlier complaint against him and discovered he had been cheating on his reported financials. We had a very thorough interview covering all these matters, with two of my staff members joining us. We presented detailed proof of all the charges.

Then I said, "You are not a match for our company. We have two choices. We can resolve this in court or you can sell your market center to someone that we approve in the next thirty days. The choice is yours."

He responded plaintively, "Mo, you're a Christian and you have to forgive me."

"Well, I would if I heard a sincere apology."

The man proceeded to offer his apology, which sounded sincere.

I then said, "I forgive you. Now, we can resolve this in one of two ways," and repeated the options I'd given before. I forgave him personally, but held him accountable to the standards he had violated. This is my practical sense of what tough love means.

I want to honor my mother for giving me a tough love role model. She loved all her children, but she was tough. She expected us to do what she asked and live up to our Christian values. When we didn't, she let us know right away. My father was easy on us, but my mother was tough. Thank you, Mom—your example made me a better leader.

Doing the right thing is not always the easy way, but it is the best way. I have learned over the years that every employee and agent must be responsible for guarding our reputation. Tough love is often necessary to drive that home. To be a leader in anything you do, you will need to build on the foundational idea of tough love. You will gain the confidence of others and for yourself. Be a tough love leader.

MO-MENTUM BUILDERS

» Be determined and act now—if you delay discipline, behavior only gets worse.

» As a leader, become a keeper and defender of the culture. Doing the right thing is not always the easiest way, but it is the best way.

» If people begin to call you "the velvet hammer" or something similar, take it as a compliment. It means they see that you care and that you hold to standards.

» Remember that adults, as well as children, need boundaries. They feel secure when they know the rules.

» Handling conflict just comes with the job if one is in leadership. People are going to push the boundaries and test your commitment to the standards.

» Use the three strikes option. It gives everyone an opportunity to change. If they don't, they have made the decision for you.

» Use the "tough love sandwich" method. Being tough in the middle is acceptable to others when it is surrounded with love.

15

Lesson:

PROFIT MATTERS

"A great business has a purpose to serve and to deliver something valuable to its clients and customers. But profit is the measure of the business's health and its ability to last."

In my experience, many people don't really understand the concept of profit. They listen to those who associate it with greed and selfishness. They have heard politicians, talking heads, and investigative reporters ridicule the lifestyles of the rich and famous. They have often come to associate profit with excess and immorality. Profit is not any of that. It is a simple, common-sense financial concept: earn more than you spend. People who can do that are able to grow their wealth.

Imagine my intrigue as an 8-year-old girl when one day my dad pulled our old car in front of a stately building in downtown Enid, Oklahoma. The words engraved at the top of the building read: Carnegie Library. My dad said, "I always want you to respect the wealthy, because the wealthy can give back."

He went on to tell me the story of Andrew Carnegie: He made his money in steel and then wanted to give it all away before he died. Among many other contributions, he gave towns and villages all across America the money to build libraries and fill them with books. The lesson of Andrew Carnegie would stay with me for a lifetime.

I understand that people may choose to use their money or spend their wealth in frivolous and extravagant ways. They may even use it to do things that we would consider immoral. But, that is about them and their values. It does not define profit or wealth. Our government, many businesses, and even our citizens would be well-served to understand that profit matters.

Here's what always seemed like common sense to me. Work, or operate, in such a way that what you bring in is more than what you spend. If we are not making a profit, we are going into debt. If we don't correct the situation, we will be out of business or bankrupt. There is a price to pay for overspending, for not understanding the idea of profit.

My mom and dad were not wealthy, but they understood the value of money, the importance of being thrifty, and the importance of saving and growing your wealth when you could. They knew that they couldn't live beyond their means. They had to make do with what they had or find a way to earn more. When there was a family need for something special, my dad would go find extra work so that he could buy it. I learned how challenging it was for him to budget for equipment and seeds and supplies. If it was a bad year for growing crops, the challenge became greater. My mom was a miracle worker in terms of making the most of what we had. She created wonderful meals from the least of ingredients. She made all sorts of things, including our clothes, so that we didn't have to go buy them in a store. We couldn't afford to.

Now, I'm sharing this with you not to gain your sympathy, but to help you understand what I mean when I say to you, "Profit matters!" I want you to realize, as I do, that how you treat money will impact the quality of your life and your business.

Being profitable means a business is healthy. I don't believe, as some might, that profit is the purpose of business. A great business has a purpose to serve and to deliver something valuable to its clients and customers. But profit is the measure of the business's health and its ability to last. At Keller Williams, we believe it is our mission "to build careers worth having, businesses worth owning, and lives worth living." We do that for our real estate associates and our office owners. Their purpose is to give great service to their real estate buyers, sellers, and investors. But, if we aren't profitable, we won't be able to serve. No profit, no purpose. It's that simple.

When I became president and CEO, Keller Williams Realty was essentially incubating out of a network of profitable real estate sales offices that Gary owned. The overall company was profitable but the new franchise division was not. It was, of course, in its start-up phase, and we faced plenty of challenges. Many of our franchise offices were either unproductive, unprofitable, or underperforming. Our fee and royalty structure did not generate adequate revenue. So, we took action. We restructured the income streams and worked to ensure our franchisees had every possible opportunity to be successful.

Because we cared so deeply about the success of our office owners, we put a huge emphasis on education geared to teaching profitability. In Keller Williams, our formula was simple—we taught our owners to "lead with revenues, not expenses," to "run lean and mean," and to "budget and track all your numbers." One of our advantages was that we had the KW profit-sharing system. That meant that more than 40 percent of all the profits of all our offices went into a profit share pool that was distributed every month to those who had helped us grow and become profitable.

Having that system in place meant that we had to be accountable for its performance. So, we built a culture of accountability around tracking income, expenses, and profitability of every office, every month. We made training and consulting the basis of our business relationship. This was important for them as owners and important to all our associates because of profit sharing.

I also was tough in managing the expenses of our corporate office and the franchise division. In my third year as CEO, the franchise division became profitable and then the financial numbers began to accelerate. By the time I stepped out of my CEO role and became vice chairman of the board, the company was very profitable.

Also, during my years as CEO, annual profit sharing through our franchises grew from $982,000 in 1996 to $48.5 million in 2005. And because these franchise owners were focused on profit, they were able to share those profits.

Successful men, women, and companies drive our economy, create jobs, and provide benefits for millions. I respect those who have succeeded and built their wealth. Even when I was poor, and again when I was nearly bankrupt, I never resented them. I may have, as a young girl, been jealous or envious of others because of what they had, but I never thought they were bad people or should give their money to me.

Because of our free enterprise system, people have the opportunity to rise to the top. Their hard work, creative inventions, and successful companies serve all citizens. In my opinion, the free enterprise system will only remain strong so long as we support the creative, driven individuals who make something from nothing, provide for themselves, and create products and services that benefit us all.

I knew a checker at our local Walmart by the name of Olivia. I learned that she was going to retire soon, so one day I asked, "Are you going to be okay in your retirement?"

She smiled and answered, "Well, do you think $2 million will be okay?"

I was stunned and happy for her at the same time. Not bad for a checker, huh? When folks badmouth Walmart, I think of Olivia. Walmart gave her the opportunity to exercise her stock options and she did. Now she is retiring with financial independence.

Oil companies get a lot of scrutiny and criticism as well. Don't say anything bad about oil companies to me; I grew up in the oil patch. Oil companies do things for our communities that would just blow you away. And their business fluctuates greatly. Some years they make billions of dollars and some years they lose billions.

I am also a huge fan of anyone who wants to build a business of their own. It is a passion of mine to promote entrepreneurship.

The lesson Dad taught me sitting in front of the Carnegie Library was this: don't ridicule or judge those with wealth; instead, be grateful for what they can do and the needs they can meet for those less fortunate. Pray they use their wealth wisely and are led to help the poor, the sick, and those around the world who can't help themselves.

Here's what I now truly appreciate about profit and wealth. It brings with it great opportunity to do good for others. As a wealthy person, I feel so blessed and grateful that I want to do everything I can to enrich the lives of others. For instance, Richard and I have established the Gregg Foundation, in honor of my mother and father, to benefit care for the elderly. I can do it, I should do it, and I want to do it.

I truly believe that no matter our circumstances, each of us can still make a difference to many by giving a portion of what we earn. I encourage our Keller Williams associates to tithe. God promises to bless such giving. Think of it. If everyone were committed to giving a tenth of their income, we wouldn't need a welfare system. Churches and religious institutions would have the funds necessary to care for orphans, widows, the elderly, the sick, and the infirmed. Even the smallest of children can learn to give a penny out of every dime.

In Keller Williams, our associates and business owners not only celebrate the distribution of their profits on the twenty-first of every month, but they continually sponsor their own local fund-raising events. Everyone's hard work ultimately culminates with a system-wide "RED Day" every year in May, a powerful idea created by Cory Older, a member of our KWRI team. On RED Day, every region and every office in our company focuses on doing charitable works in their local communities. The results are both breathtaking and heartwarming.

In 2003, we established KW Cares, a nonprofit that serves the emergency needs of Keller Williams associates. It was a program started by Mary Tennant and her wonderful associate leadership council in our Austin Southwest market center. They had originally organized themselves to help colleagues that were sick or facing hardships—things like delivering food when someone was sick or providing rides when a vehicle broke down—in the spirit of "family helping family." Before long, they were holding fund-raisers and addressing bigger and bigger challenges in their office community. When you understand that these were all independent contractors competing for the same buyers and sellers, you can see what a powerful cultural statement it was. What Mary and her team started, I shepherded to our growing company.

Just two years later in 2005, KW Cares raised and distributed more than $5.3 million to support the victims of Hurricane Katrina along the Gulf Coast. Since its inception, more than 2,400 grants totaling over $21 million have been given, including tithes to board-approved organizations that share a similar mission.

Our annual Family Reunion ends each year with an Inspirational Breakfast where we honor those people onstage who are doing wonderful, charitable things. We highlight their work and whenever possible gift them a substantial donation to continue their good work. It is humbling to watch as additional money is raised immediately by the thousands of associates who attend. Quite simply, it is a big-time passing of the hat. And, there is great energy and joy in the room.

In my experience, those who have earned a profit are also willing to share it. Being profitable and being generous just seem to go hand in hand. I have been truly touched at the spirit of giving that comes from those who are working to be profitable. I respect the value of every human being, no matter what their economic situation. And, I have deep empathy for those who are disadvantaged, disabled, and oppressed. I believe that we all must find ways to help those who are truly in need. But, we won't accomplish this by judging the wealthy or creating resentment for them. They have not caused the problems of the poor and they have the greatest capacity for helping them. Not because they are forced to, but because they are encouraged to do what they can and appreciated for what they do.

In my experience, those who have earned a profit are also willing to share it. Being profitable and being generous just seem to go hand in hand.

My father's lesson that day long ago on a street outside the Carnegie Library found a place in my heart and mind. It instilled an appreciation for the opportunities and responsibilities of those who have been blessed with much. I have made it my focus to use my blessings to help others. Though I may never be able to bless others with a library in every town, I will continue to give out of my abundance.

As an adult, I came to understand that wealth represents the opportunity of a free enterprise system. It is this economic system that has been the foundation of our great American republic. It has given us a prosperity that so many in the rest of the world admire and seek to attain for themselves. We all have the same freedom and opportunity as the wealthy—to work hard, work smart, be of service, and earn our own wealth. As my dad said: "Respect the wealthy." Don't judge them. They have helped make our lives better and our country great.

What makes all of this generosity and giving possible is profit. Ultimately, I want to teach people that profit matters not for its own sake, but for what it enables us to do—for our families, for our communities, and for the world. In the end, it isn't about how much money you make; it's about all the lives you will touch. In your business and in your life, earn more than you spend or spend less than you earn. Either way, the difference makes a difference. It allows you to prosper and build wealth. When you have that, you not only provide financial security for your family; you now have the opportunity to make a difference with others. Profit matters!

MO-MENTUM BUILDERS

» Focus on being profitable—it matters.

» Profit is not the purpose of a business; it is a measure of its health.

» Spend less than you bring in—that is what profit is. In business, lead with revenues, not expenses. Budget everything and stay within the budget.

» Remember the guidance of my father: "Respect the wealthy; the wealthy can give back." In fact, be grateful for those blessed enough financially to make a difference in the lives of others.

» Those who aren't profitable don't have money to share.

» Help others learn the importance of profit and financial discipline.

» Do your best, work hard, work smart, and be of service to others. If you are blessed with wealth and abundance, then use it to give back and make a difference in the world.

» Commit to tithing. Remember, if everyone were willing to give a tenth of their income to those in need, we wouldn't require a welfare system.

» Don't judge those with wealth—aspire to be one of them.

» Don't judge those who are poor—aspire to be able to help them.

Mo and brother, Lee, growing up on the farm in Oklahoma.

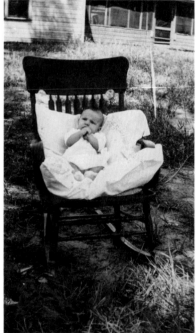

Top Mo as a child sledding on the farm during the winter.

Bottom *(L)* Mo as a baby in 1937. *(R)* Gregg family: John, Audra, Felix, Lee, Mo, and Faith.

Top (L) Mo as a teenager with her parents, John and Audra Gregg. *(R)* Mo in grade school growing up on the farm.

Bottom Mo driving the tractor, wearing a feed sack dress sewn by her mother.

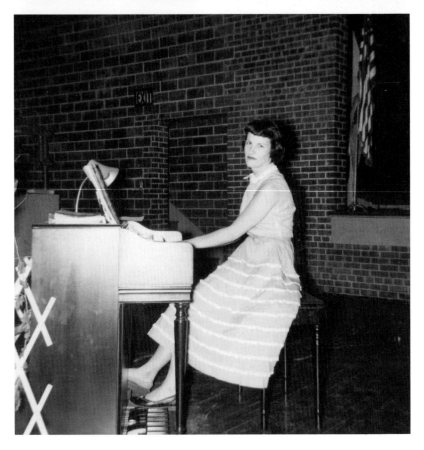

Top (L) Richard, high school senior. *(R)* Mo, high school senior.
Bottom Mo playing piano in a school concert.

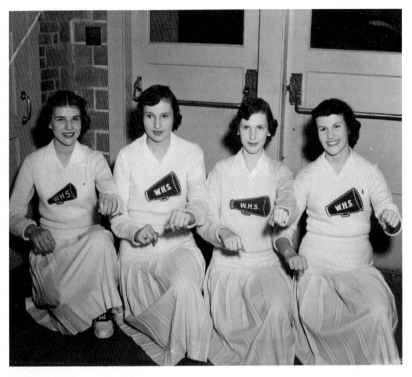

Top Mo at Waukomis High School, cheerleader.

Bottom *(L)* Mo in high school, FFA queen (Future Farmers of America).
(R) Mo and her cousin after World War II.

Top 1957, Richard and Mo's wedding.

Bottom 1962, Anderson family: Richard, Rick, Mo, and Karin.

Top Mo during her early real estate career in Oklahoma.

Bottom Richard and Mo at a Century 21 convention, 1983.

Mo in her first real estate office, Titan Realtors, owned with Ruth Honeycutt and Jerry Brown.

16

Lesson:

LOVE YOUR COUNTRY

"We must think bigger, like the founding fathers of this country did. We must find a way to work together to solve the major issues facing our country."

I am unashamedly patriotic to the core. My love for America and our way of life runs deep and I would defend our freedom with my life. When my brother left home to serve in World War II, it was a tough time for our family, but every American was committed to help in any way possible. We used ration stamps issued by the government, bought bonds, and helped with "support our troops" efforts.

Sugar was a scarce commodity so we used it sparingly. There were times Mom used our only sugar to make cookies and sweets for the soldiers passing through on outward-bound trains. My parents and I would drive to the depot in Drummond and wait for the trains carrying soldiers. As the trains pulled to a brief stop, we would motion for soldiers to lower their windows so we could hand them the fresh-baked cookies or other goodies Mom had made. You should have seen their faces light up.

I came to know the truths and values on which our country was founded better when I first went to Girls State. That experience allowed me to understand the processes of American government. Serving as mayor of a created town piqued my interest in leadership and politics.

I am what is referred to as a conservative. I am also a Christian. By putting those two words together, Christian conservative, I am aware that some will label me "politically incorrect." However, for me, the word conservative simply means one who "conserves," "keeps guard," or "closely observes." Although sometimes I get discouraged with the way our country is being run today, I deeply love the truths it was built on and the values it stands for.

I especially appreciate our free enterprise system, which has allowed a tenant farmer's daughter, like me, to succeed and have such an abundant life. And when I got into the real estate business, I came to appreciate that one of the most precious aspects of our democracy is the freedom and opportunity for citizens to own their own homes. In my mid-30s, we bought our first home. What a difference it made. That spot of land was my kingdom—mine! There are countries in the world where one might be able to own the bricks and mortar of a home, but not the land beneath it. Our democracy gives us the right and privilege of complete ownership of our property. It makes my heart sing to see the look of joy on the faces of others who have closed on the purchase of their first home. It is proof they have reached an important milestone in life. For most people, home ownership is the "American Dream."

I also count the right to vote as one of our most precious freedoms. I could hardly wait to reach 21 and be qualified to vote. Now, of course, the voting age is 18. I still remember the first time I stood in a voting booth. I felt a deep satisfaction that comes from having a voice in the direction and policies of our nation. My candidate may not win every election, but I do my part in determining the outcome. Voting is a sign of patriotism, just like standing for "The Star-Spangled Banner" with my hand over my heart. It is what true patriots do.

Nearly half of our population doesn't vote for various reasons: "I didn't have time; I was confused about the candidates; I wasn't informed enough about the issues; it doesn't matter who is elected—all politicians are the same." The excuse that rankles me most is "My vote won't make a difference." The fact is that the only way you can make a difference is by voting.

Many believe our political system is broken. I don't believe it is completely broken, but it sure is in need of repair. We must think bigger, like the founding fathers of this country did. We must find a way to work together to solve the major issues facing our country.

My real concern is that our principles and founding values are not being taught in school anymore. The U.S. Constitution is often misrepresented, and many children no longer understand how the framework of our nation was established. They don't realize that our founding fathers believed in a limited government whose primary job was to protect the rights and freedoms of the individual.

I know I'm outspoken. My husband Richard reminds me that, "Most people don't want to really say what they think for fear it might offend someone." But I know that outspoken debate was a healthy part of our founding fathers' conventions. They studied the lessons of very learned men, debated the issues vehemently, and then laid down the fundamentals of our great democratic society.

After some of my outspoken moments, people say, "Mo, you need to be the President." I laugh and tell them if I got elected, I'd probably be impeached in my first week. I do know that I'm not qualified for that high office, but if I were President, the first thing I'd do is cut the budget and make sure we lived within it. Beyond that, I would have a fireside chat with the American people each month to teach and discuss the principles of the Constitution. I would have brilliant, respected people on hand to educate Americans on our fundamental rights and responsibilities. We would take time to discuss our basic founding principles. Because that is how I have led every organization I've been a part of, and it has always produced powerful results.

I admired President Ronald Reagan for bringing people together. Patriotic pride was at an all-time high because he made us believe we were the greatest nation on earth. He didn't engage in class warfare, but talked about a cohesive, united country. He also talked about his faith openly and spoke of his dependence on God. His rhetoric was simple and heartfelt. Reagan was a powerful leader respected by both parties. Today, we are desperately yearning for leaders who will tell us the truth and bring us together.

My life—from a tenant farm in the Dust Bowl to the boardroom of a world-class company, and my path from poverty to financial independence—is a testament to the fact that America is truly a land of opportunity. I pray we never take for granted our great country and that we never forget we are "one nation under God." Be grateful for where you live, the freedoms you have, and the opportunities it grants you. Love your country!

MO-MENTUM BUILDERS

- » Be sure to vote. Voting is a sign of patriotism. It is what true patriots do.

- » Help renew our political system and our government. It may not be completely broken, but it sure is in need of repair.

- » Be grateful for where you live, the freedoms you have, and the opportunities it grants you.

17

Lesson:

LOVE YOUR NEIGHBOR

"Throughout my lifetime, including the years of serving in leadership for Keller Williams, I have held the belief that treating people equally and fairly is an important element of a values-based culture."

The New Testament tells of an encounter Christ once had with a lawyer who asked, "What can I do to inherit eternal life?"

Christ pointed the man to the scripture that says, "You shall love the Lord your God with all your heart, with all your soul, with all your strength, and all your mind, and *your neighbor as yourself.*"

To which the lawyer asked, "And who is my neighbor?"

Then Christ told the story of the Good Samaritan in order to explain that our neighbors are other human beings all around us, especially those in need.

My father was the first to visit any neighbor who was sick or in need of help. He didn't have money to offer, but he found other ways to help. He stopped in to check on widows left behind after their husbands passed away. He volunteered to plow their fields. He harvested crops for friends who were ill or short of hands. He would show up to do chores and various household repairs for those facing hard times. My dad's unselfish, caring actions will remain in my memory for a lifetime.

Dad was so generous he picked up every hitch-hiker he saw along the highway and fed every hobo showing up at our door. In those days, many out-of-work homeless men would ride the trains, then jump off at every community to go door-to-door asking for work or food. I'm sure word got around that our farm was the place to go for a hot meal.

Once a month our family would make a trip into Enid to buy supplies. Dad couldn't have had much money, yet he never failed to toss some coins into the hats of the men who sat or stood outside the stores asking for help. When it was butchering time on the farm, after stocking our smokehouse, Dad set aside some of the meat to share with neighbors or friends. I'm sure for him it was like giving a tithe.

When I was a child, our neighbors were Al and Vera Kenner, an African-American couple with children who lived a mile down the road from us. Al farmed with Dad and we often had them over for dinner. My family never saw them as "different" in the least. In fact, when Al would take a load of wheat over to the grain elevator, I often rode along with him in his truck. Once I looked at Al's hand on the steering wheel as he drove and said, "Al, why do you have a better suntan than I do?"

He explained simply, yet profoundly, and his answer has stayed with me all these years. "Well," Al answered, "God loves color, so he made white people, brown people, yellow people, and black people, like me."

Everyone in our rural community loved Al and his family, respected their hard work, and shared their family values. We were neighbors and we were friends.

As I grew up I could never understand racial prejudice of any kind.

Dr. Alan Robson was one of the first coaches in Oklahoma to include a black player on his basketball team. Richard and I watched as the opposing teams, their fans, and even referees treated that young man terribly. It would make me livid when they called him names, ridiculed his play, or taunted him in other ways. Dr. Robson would immediately address such actions, defending the young man, and making a public stand.

Later, when I interviewed for a teaching job in Ponca City, I had the opportunity to personally tell Dr. Robson, who had become the school superintendent of the city, how I admired his actions in defense of that man.

Throughout my lifetime, including the years of serving in leadership for Keller Williams, I have held the belief that treating people equally and fairly is an important element of a values-based culture. During my entire teaching and business career, I could not and would not tolerate prejudice.

When I helped launch the Inspirational Breakfast for our KW Family Reunion, I wanted it to be an all-inclusive spiritual highlight of our time together. Many people told me how much they liked the event and the ways it touched them personally. They were so impressed that a big business like Keller Williams Realty would bring a spiritual dimension to their annual convention.

I made sure that all the major religions were represented, and that a KW family member of each of those faiths would offer a prayer, in their own unique way, at the opening of the program. But, along the way, I became aware of a few Christians who were expressing disappointment that we would allow a Buddhist or a Muslim or a Hindu to take an active part in the event.

When they conveyed this disappointment to me personally, I responded firmly, "You know what? I've been a Christian a long time. I believe in Jesus. You don't have to worry about my Christianity, my commitment, or my theology. But I know this deep in my heart: Jesus himself taught us to be loving to all and welcoming to all. That is what we are doing with this event: being hospitable and recognizing that people are free to choose their own faith."

When I talked to my trusted friend Ravi Zacharias about this negative feedback, he responded with a gentle laugh and said, "You're doing exactly the right thing, Mo. As Christians we embrace Jews, Hindus, Muslims, Buddhists, because, though we may not agree with their theology, we love them as Christ loves them. Building a bridge does not mean surrendering ground."

The goal of our Inspirational Breakfast is to embrace everyone and create lasting memories as we encourage our people to give, to care, and to "love your neighbor as yourself."

If ever there was a man who loved his neighbor as himself, it was my dad. I grew to understand that my neighbor is not just the family next door, but anyone in need around the world. How different our world would be if every human being made that a daily goal. Love your neighbor.

MO-MENTUM BUILDERS

» Treat others with courtesy, hospitality, and respect. We are all human beings and worthy of God's love.

» Do not tolerate prejudice and bigotry. Be above that in all you do.

» Know that when you treat others fairly and with respect, it will return to you.

» Love your neighbor. How different our world would be if every human being made that a daily goal.

» Understand that your neighbor is not just the family next door, but all the people around the world.

18

Lesson:

KEEP RELATIONSHIPS FOR LIFE

"A cup of coffee with someone you care about is therapeutic and can make a difference. Think about special things you can do to lift someone's spirit or encourage them. Give a gift to someone you are thinking about."

In 2006, after serving ten years as CEO, I stepped down from the top position at Keller Williams to become vice chairman of the board. I realized that I was truly exhausted from working so hard and so long. I was feeling it physically as well as mentally. At my age, it was time to do some other things I wanted to do, like spending more time with Richard and making memories with my grandchildren. It was also time to take care of my health. I intend to live past 100, like my dear friend Ebby Halliday, the iconic real estate leader in Dallas.

As I began to relax a bit and had some quiet time to myself, I reflected on my life and what I had accomplished. I thought about how it all happened, and I concluded that the wonderful relationships in my life had made all the difference.

I'm sure it goes back to memories of simpler times, but I get nostalgic for the kind of relationships with friends and neighbors I knew as a child. In those days, contact had to be personal; there were no cell phones or email. Neighbors talked across the fence to one another, sat on the front porch visiting with friends in the cool of the evening, shared the bounty of their gardens, and checked on each other's houses when families were away. In short, people looked out for one another.

Perhaps my upbringing is the reason I make it a point to stay in contact with old friends and also make new friends along the way.

Richard and I make sure to attend all our school reunions. Our tiny high school had a graduating class of only seventeen. Richard is building a barn on our property in Waukomis to serve as an event center where we can hold our future reunions. Each year Richard and I drive to Ponca City to see friends we made more than fifty years ago. We love reconnecting with each other. Once a year, I take twelve of my old classmates from the Oklahoma College for Women (now called USAO) on a surprise weekend. What wonderful friendships I enjoy with these women; friendships formed when we were all just young girls.

There is not time nor space to write of the many people Richard and I have met and appreciated in our lives, but another special group is made up of those I worked with early in my real estate business. Longtime friends like Jerry Brown and Ruth Honeycutt who invested in our first real estate office. Business partners like Gary Keller, Mark Willis, Mary Tennant, John Davis, and Chris Heller to whom I owe so much. As often as possible I want to see these people, maintain our friendships, and thank them for the "bucket filling" they have done in my life.

After moving to Austin to begin my stint as CEO, I wanted to stay connected to my friends in Oklahoma City, so I invited them to Austin for a special weekend.

Even though I was busy and a bit overwhelmed with my new job, I made time to plan every detail. I wanted to create a time so memorable that the ladies would look forward to getting together year after year.

We all stayed in my little apartment. It was cramped, some had to sleep on the floor, but we had a great time. I took them to events and sites in Austin including the State Capitol. We enjoyed Esther's Follies, a comedic, musical theater in the Vaudeville tradition, and then spent an evening at The Oasis, a beautiful restaurant on Lake Travis. Every evening there was a gift left on each pillow; small, simple tokens of my love for each one. It is all about staying connected.

I encourage you to make time to enjoy friends and family as much as possible. You don't have to spend a lot of money doing it. Have your best friends meet you some Saturday afternoon and take a walk. Every city has places you can meet: parks, nature centers, museums. A cup of coffee with someone you care about is therapeutic and can make a difference. Think about special things you can do to lift someone's spirit or encourage them. Give a gift to someone you are thinking about. It doesn't have to be elaborate: a bookmark, a card, a scripture verse you want to share. The important point is that you are giving them the most precious gift—your time.

The person who has given me the most in life is my husband, Richard. I am eternally grateful for him. Richard is more of a private person than me. He could live in a cabin somewhere in Colorado, and if he had C-SPAN and his books, he'd be perfectly happy. He loves people but is not a social creature like me. He retreats to his office in our home and spends time on our Waukomis property because he actually enjoys being alone. He is such a gentle spirit.

Someday I want to write a book about marriages that last. Ours has lasted fifty-seven years, so I think Richard and I have discovered some secrets. He has always been supportive; he is proud of the woman I am, and I couldn't have accomplished anything without his insight and guidance. Throughout our marriage Richard has helped me see things more clearly. I've learned from him. He has been a huge part of every major decision I've ever made; I trust him completely.

Relationships with our children and grandchildren are most precious. As we grow older, Richard and I realize we have a limited time to make memories with them. We often have our grandchildren over for Grandkids Dinner and we make it a special time. When we invite them, we tell them ahead of time what we will be talking about. We ask them to prepare questions and to be ready to discuss them. The topics have included sports, presidents, University of Oklahoma football, and places in the world they would like to visit. I have fulfilled the promise to take each grandchild anywhere they want to go in the world, as long as it's safe. What great memories we have of those trips.

Maintaining lifelong relationships is not always easy. You have to work at it and realize now how much it will mean to you later. Friendship has no boundaries of age, time, or place. Even a brother, a sister, a husband, a father, or a grandchild can be a good friend. Some relationships I treasure have even developed during difficult circumstances in my life. When each circumstance was solved, the friendship remained. The special relationships I enjoy are based on acceptance, honesty, and a shared desire to stay connected.

In a world full of uncertainties, it is wonderful to know there are people who have your best interest at heart, those whom you can call at 4:00 in the morning with a problem, those who will tell you the truth even when it hurts. Henry David Thoreau said, "Be true to your work, your word, and your friends."

I thank God for every meaningful relationship in my life. I am a rich woman because I have my family and friends. I have relationships for life!

MO-MENTUM BUILDERS

» Each day in your quiet time, ask God to direct you or impress you with someone you can touch. Then act on that guidance.

» You will grow to deeply appreciate relationships that endure.

» Have a cup of coffee with someone you care about. It will be therapeutic for both of you and can make a difference for each of you.

» Think about special things you can do to lift someone's spirit or encourage them. Give a small, thoughtful gift to someone you are thinking about.

» Maintaining lifelong relationships takes work and intention. It is not always easy. In the end, you will be very glad you did.

» Keep relationships for life. They will be your most valuable possessions.

19

Lesson:

ACCEPT THAT YOU WILL BE TESTED

"I believe that when we are tested,

we have the greatest opportunity to

grow and learn and become stronger."

I was tempted to leave this lesson out. Most of the lessons I've shared have been upbeat and positive. This one is too, but in a very different way. I want to talk with you about the dark times, the times of self-doubt, and the times when life throws you a curveball, maybe even a knuckleball. You will be tested.

I don't think it's always God's intention. I just think it's the way He designed it. We have free will. We can make choices about what we do. And, the world will respond. There will be consequences. Part of our learning as we mature is coming to terms with this. We begin to truly understand the consequences of our actions. We learn to take responsibility and be accountable. We also learn how things work and how to make the best of it.

I believe that when we are tested, we have the greatest opportunity to grow and learn and become stronger. I know that has been true for me. Those difficult early days in the Dust Bowl taught me so many of my most enduring lessons, as I've shared with you. And, they gave me the chance to build boldness and courage that an easier childhood might not have. I also got to watch my own father and mother face those times with courage, faith, and gratitude.

And the tests will always be there, no matter how old we are or how well off. Life will give us another opportunity to show our poise, our fortitude, and our tenacity.

That lesson was never more clear to me than on April 18, 2008. Four years before, in 2004, Richard and I started the process of designing and building our dream home. Remember, this was one of my first childhood dreams: to own a lovely, elegant home. Property was purchased in the vicinity of Edmond, and we scheduled initial meetings with Austin designer Betty Shaw.

In August of 2006, ground was broken and the dream was on its way to becoming a reality. Matt Wilson would be the main builder and his construction supervisor, Thomas Shaw, would handle all the related details of construction. Thomas estimated the home would be completely finished and ready for us in August of 2008. We could hardly wait!

As spring of 2008 approached, we were excited because it looked as if the builders were a little ahead of schedule. The house was 90 percent complete already. We had all our plans to move in and to begin inviting our family and friends to come share this magnificent new home . . . my dream home.

Then came April 18. It started as just another ordinary day.

I was on a plane returning to the United States after a visit to the Holy Land, and Richard was staying at our

Walnut Cove home. He woke up that morning to the phone ringing. He could hardly take in the grim news. Our beautiful home had been totally destroyed due to a lightning strike the night before. Lightning had started a fire that burned for more than eight hours, destroying all but a small portion of the exterior. The intense heat even compromised the foundation. Richard was shaken and tried to phone me right away, but I was in-flight and could not be reached. During my layover in Dallas, in route to Oklahoma City, Richard informed me of the unbelievable loss over the phone.

"The house is a complete loss, Mo. It's all gone." Richard spoke slowly, deliberately, giving me time to process the tragic report.

I couldn't. I was devastated. Through my tears I asked God, "Why? What have we done to deserve this? Haven't we tried to honor You and now the home we wanted to share with others as a testimony to Your goodness is nothing but rubble?"

I cried throughout the flight to Oklahoma City. Then my heart was broken again later that day as we stood along the street with fire fighters, police officers, family, and friends who gathered at the site of the fire. The subcontractors wept along with us. This had been a labor of love for them for nearly two years. Now, there was nothing but smoldering, broken pieces jutting up in ugly, charred spikes; piles of ashes everywhere.

Richard and I tried to focus on the good out of the tragedy. No one was in the house, so no one was injured. We had not moved in as yet, so personal belongings, family heirlooms, and most of our furniture had not been lost. An antique French fireplace, made of hand-carved Carrara marble in the 1860s, had been removed from the house the day before the fire. We knew the bricks and mortar of the home could be rebuilt, but we mourned the loss of a dream nearly in our grasp. We carried such deep heartbreak that we considered not rebuilding.

It was a testing time. I thought maybe it was a sign that we shouldn't be building such a luxurious place, that it was not right with God. Richard and I prayed about it. We spent many hours talking. I could feel that my dream was still there. I really wanted to build it and share it with all those I care about. I've been in real estate for decades; I knew it was a good investment that would hold its value for generations.

In the end, we came to understand that it was a simple act of nature. We also knew that the dream persisted; the dream had not been destroyed in the fire. We believed that God had called us to build a home that would serve greater purposes than we even imagined. So, with a new determination, we gave the approval to begin construction again. Three months after the fire, on July 15, the old foundation slab was removed and a new foundation was laid. The project would take another two years to complete.

It was May 3, 2010, when Richard and I moved into Stonemill II, our lovely dream home that I described in lesson #2. We may never know the purpose of losing the first home until we see God face to face, but I know this: we were more grateful, more joyous, and more committed than ever before to dedicate the home to

God for purposes that would bring glory and honor to Him. Perhaps we had passed a test and had earned the right to enjoy the dream home at a whole new level.

A point of comfort to me is the message engraved in stone on the front porch entry. It is a verse from Psalms 127:1, "Unless the Lord builds the house, its builders labor in vain." Indeed, God built this house. This house, everything in it and around it, belongs to Him. He just lets Richard and me borrow it for a while and live here. We are stewards of the things God has given us to enjoy.

Soon after the fire destroyed Stonemill I, our daughter Karin and grandson Conner were looking through the debris. They found a charred piece of wood in the shape of a cross. For as long as I live I will remember how they excitedly carried the cross to me and Conner's words, "Look, Grammy, God still loves you. We found a cross." We framed that cross and it is displayed in our home as a symbol of God's eternal grace and mercy.

We have already hosted so many groups and events here at Stonemill; I can't recall all of them. Our home has been a meeting place for fund-raising galas, charity events, ministry organizations, Bible study groups, athletic teams (we hosted the women's basketball team from the University of Oklahoma along with Coach Sherri Coale not long ago), civic clubs including the Edmond Chamber of Commerce, and scores of holiday dinners and parties with family and friends.

I often wonder what my parents would have thought about this grand home. Both passed away in 1982.

They lived to see our first business succeed, but were not alive to see me take the CEO position at Keller Williams. They thought the house we lived in for thirty years before Stonemill was the most beautiful home in the world. They might see Stonemill and think, "This is too much, too extravagant. You could have given the money spent on this house to missions." I would understand. They lived such simple lives and Stonemill is not a simple place. However, deep down, I think they would be proud and happy for me.

Of course, the loss of our dream home was not the first time we had been tested in life. I've already mentioned our losses in the late '80s. That was a tough test! Watching our hard-earned savings disappear was both tragic and overwhelming. We shed many tears and endured many sleepless nights, wondering how we would survive. But survive we did and found ourselves more blessed than ever.

When I reached my 70s, I thought I'd be pretty much settled and wouldn't have major trials, no bumps in the road. That wasn't the case. Besides the fire, there have been other personal trials Richard and I had to walk through. In fact, just four months after the fire, Richard had emergency brain surgery to remove two subdural hematomas; and then two months after that he had open-heart surgery. Tests don't go away just because you get to be 77 years old; they are part of life.

Tests don't go away just because you get to be 77 years old; they are part of life.

In my life, during all the tests I have faced, the most powerful step I have learned to take is a very simple one: take everything to God in prayer. Leave the burden, the anger, and the pain in His hands. I have learned to turn it over to Him because I am not smart enough, good enough, or powerful enough to handle these things on my own.

I do one other thing that helps me get through tough times. I do what Abraham did in the Old Testament. On every occasion when God performed a miracle or answered a prayer, Abraham built an altar to commemorate the wonderful thing God did. When he faced other trials, Abraham could look back at those altars, because they were great reminders of God's faithfulness and His great love.

I do the same thing in my mind. I build altars of remembrance as to how God has never failed me. It gives me hope and a "peace that passes all understanding." And, it helps me get through the testing times.

There will be tests. Accept them. Even welcome them. They are such great teachers. And, I know you will grow from them.

MO–MENTUM BUILDERS

- ⇒ Embrace what life brings you. If it is difficult, you can use it to grow stronger. If it is confusing, you can use it to grow wiser. If it is discouraging, you can use it to build your courage and faith.

- ⇒ Don't expect life to be easy. When it is, enjoy those times. When it isn't, just treat it as expected. No need for panic or anger. Stay calm and look for the opportunity it is presenting.

- ⇒ Take all things to God in prayer. If you open your heart and listen carefully, you will know what to do.

- ⇒ Count your blessings. Gratitude is the attitude of the resilient.

20

Lesson:

CONNECT THE DOTS

"It's like a game of connect the dots. You don't see it in the beginning, but when all the dots are connected, an image is revealed—one you didn't see when you started."

I am 77 years old now and experiencing the happiest days of my life. One day recently, Richard was expressing the ways in which God has blessed us.

"You know," he said, "even the little, seemingly insignificant things that happen to us are all part of a grander scheme God has in mind for each one of us. It's like a game of connect the dots. You don't see it in the beginning, but when all the dots are connected, an image is revealed—one you didn't see when you started."

My life is coming full circle, and I now grasp the pattern of all the dots. Richard is right. What I can now see clearly wasn't at all clear to me while I was living in each dot. Some of those times didn't seem like progress toward anything. In fact, they felt like times of difficulty and discouragement. But, as I look back, I can see that each one was a meaningful part of the pattern that has emerged. What a magnificent path those dots have created.

But, Richard's idea about connecting the dots has several levels to it. The first level is to simply see the highlights and mileposts of your life, how it moved from one phase to the next and led you along an interesting, sometimes surprising path. It's never a straight line. It moves along in a curvy, often loopy way. Sometimes it even doubles back on itself or requires a leap over some obstacle. But wonderfully and miraculously it leads to where you are right now. It is the journey of your life.

But I think Richard's point about "connecting the dots" goes deeper than simply looking at the milestones, even as wonderful as that exercise has been for me. What he really challenged me to do was look deeper and discover God's hand in it. To see what it meant and where it really led me. To see how the events that seemed, at the time, to be misfortunes were actually preparing me for or guiding me to something greater. To see how every challenge and difficulty was, in hindsight, actually critical to my life journey. To understand that they were a part of God's grand plan for me.

If I hadn't been raised in poverty, I might never have sought to be wealthy. And, I might not have valued it as much or been so willing to share it. If I hadn't been required to work so hard on the farm, I might not have developed the powerful work ethic and tenacity I have. If I hadn't been stopped from getting my degree in music, I might not have cherished so greatly the opportunity to teach music when it came. And, I might not have been so determined to do it well.

If I had not had such a difficult time beginning my real estate career, I might not have been so passionate about helping other agents start theirs. If I hadn't been so challenged by some of my teachers, I might not have been so good at setting high standards and insisting on people living up to them.

If Richard and I had not lost almost all of our money in the late 1980s, I wouldn't have formed Pro Development Systems, which took me to Dallas to do training for Mike Bowman, which led me to visiting a Keller Williams office, which eventually gave me the opportunity to be a part owner of a very successful business. So, there you go, from financial disaster to financial independence in one string of dots.

> *If I had not had a life full of difficult and challenging times, I would not be writing this book.*

If I had not had a life full of difficult and challenging times, I would not be writing this book. I would not have these rich and deep lessons to share with you. If my faith in God had not been challenged during my college years, I might never have met Ravi Zacharias and I might never have made such a deep commitment to trusting my life to God.

So thank you, Richard, for your wisdom. I now more deeply understand what it means to connect the dots. I so clearly see the purpose that God has for my life, the purpose he always had for my life. To be a loving leader and teacher. To build great teams and organizations that are values-driven, optimistic, and spiritual. To help people love themselves and their neighbors. To further God's work on earth.

Each "connect the dots" juncture was an opening up to God's will and purpose for my life. And, as with any "connect the dots" picture, each line and dot is needed to reveal the final image. If one of those items were missing, the image would not be complete and the path would have gone in another direction.

But, I'm not done. There are more dots leading on from here. They are yet to be revealed and I am excited to discover and experience them. Who knows, they may involve you.

Right now, I am in this wonderful dot—the joy and richness of my senior years. I love to stroll through the gardens in our backyard at Stonemill. I watch the birds from the park benches, then reach down to let the water of the creek run through my fingers. The water, like time, moves on, coursing to a destination further down the way.

Fall will soon come to Oklahoma again, bringing a change to the leaves of the trees here. They will turn to beautiful shades of gold, red, and orange. I can't help but feel the changing of seasons in my own life too.

Stonemill is lovely during the daytime, but it has a special magic in the evening. As I look out over the back yard, I remember what Will Rogers once said, "One must wait until evening to see how splendid the day has been."

I love looking back to see just how splendid all my days have been. The dots are so beautifully connected. What a joy-filled life it has been. Thank you, Lord.

MO-MENTUM BUILDERS

- ⇒ Take time to look back on your life and connect the dots. Even when you are younger, you will begin to see the map of your life. Let it unfold.

- ⇒ Remember, even the little, seemingly insignificant things that happen to you are all part of a grander scheme God has in mind for you.

- ⇒ Be yourself. Sing your song. Connect the dots that are you.

- ⇒ If I have learned anything in my 77 years, it is that I can't be someone else. God wants me to be the best Mo Anderson I can be. He wants you to be the best you that you can be.

- ⇒ Life isn't over until it's over. You can still have dreams and goals. You're never too old. Stay active, engaged, and busy. Go live more dots.

- ⇒ The difficult times are just important steps to the good times. You will only come to deeply understand that later.

- ⇒ Have faith that God has a plan for your life. He is creating the dots that will form the pattern your life was meant to have. Give yourself to His will for you.

Acknowledgments

There are so many people I want to thank for all they have done—directly or indirectly—to fulfill my *dream* of writing this book. My life, as you now know, has been blessed with wonderful mentors, partners, colleagues, family, and friends. I have collaborated with many and learned from them all. I hope I have done adequate justice in this book to their contributions to my life.

On a list of those who have been instrumental in making this book a reality, no one could be named before my beloved husband, Richard. He has been my biggest encourager, in this project as in all things. I am sure this comes as no surprise to those who know us. He is a loving, supportive, and wise confidant. Along with his positive presence, which is woven throughout the tapestry of my life and the pages of this book, Richard contributed the title. We both wholeheartedly agree, despite the challenges, this has been a *joy-filled life* together.

Always daring me to do more, "You must share with others what you know to be true and learned to do so well," he would say to me. "The world needs your message." So, thank you, Richard, for signing me up for a real estate class and urging me to write this book. With my whole heart, I love you.

Next to Richard, the most influential man in my adulthood has been Gary Keller. He has worn many hats in my life: business partner, mentor, coach, and friend. Certainly I had created success in business through my own hard work, tenacity, and initiative; however, Gary extended the invitation that catapulted my life to new heights. With a handshake, he changed my world and set me on the adventure of a lifetime—a gift for which I will be eternally grateful. In critical ways, Gary and I are very different—and, in truth, that may have been the *difference-maker* in our success together. He was the *visionary* and I was the *implementer*. Together, we formed a powerful business partnership, lifelong friendship, and a union capable of international success. I do, indeed, feel blessed beyond measure for this experience. Gary: above all else, I thank you for believing in me and for giving me the opportunity to create a life of *significance*.

I have been blessed to be surrounded by an amazing team of leaders. They have supported me, inspired me, and added to my understanding of values-based business leadership. Mark Willis, CEO, and Mary Tennant, president, succeeded me in these roles at Keller Williams Realty. Each brought his and her own unique gifts to our executive leadership that spurred exponential growth of the company.

Mark Willis took Keller Williams to the top of the real estate industry during the global economic downturn that began in 2006. Mark has a warm wit, a keen mind, and an insightful ability to understand people. This makes him a gifted communicator and, as a business executive during those recent difficult years, I was deeply grateful for Mark's unique ability to inspire positivity and to create a surge of growth when others were losing ground in our industry. More than anything else, I thank you, Mark, for the song of your hearty laughter that has echoed through our office halls for these many wonderful years in business together.

Mary Tennant is one of the finest business executives I have encountered. She has blessed Keller Williams, and my life, in ways that are beyond measure. Mary has transformed our international staff by planting in their hearts her own powerful passion for the needs of our KW associates. She is a workhorse behind the scenes, but she allows—even insists—that others receive the credit. Mary is the epitome of *servant leader*. She repeatedly said to me, "Mo, I want you to write a book. I want you to write YOUR book." Thank you, Mary, for being such a powerful proponent—and for being one of my very best friends.

Chris Heller, who has led our worldwide expansion, and John Davis, the quarterback of KW recruiting and growth, are the next generation of leadership taking the helm of Keller Williams Realty. It is my wish that, with this book, I am imparting wisdom that will be a guiding star in the night sky helping you to steer the ship into new, uncharted waters. We have never been a company that lives in the wake; rather, we use past experience to speed us forward and *onward*. I have the greatest confidence in both of you and I am grateful for the respectful, loving support that you each show for "the old lady of the company."

To Dianna Kokoszka—CEO of our MAPS Coaching division, gifted leader, precious friend, and our resident "genius"—I say thank you for the many *bold*, creative, powerful, and profitable gifts with which you have blessed our company. I cherish the years that I have known you and I am honored to be in business with you.

Next, I want to thank the talented individuals who were directly instrumental in making this book happen. Jay Papasan, vice president of publishing, along with Gary Keller, really put me on the path to writing. The many works they have produced have not only been bestsellers, they have changed the industry and impacted the lives of real estate professionals around the world. Jay has been a writing role model for me. His honesty, expertise, and invaluable feedback in my writing process have been an immeasurable blessing. With Jay's guidance, the result of my first experience as an author is a literary work that beautifully captures my voice and *sings my song loudly*. Jay, I am truly grateful.

What would I have done without the creative gifts of Annie Switt, Michael Balistreri, and Caitlin McIntosh, members of the KWRI Marketing and Communications team? Together, you make all things beautiful. The graphic design of this book truly took my breath way and brought joyful tears to my eyes when I first gazed upon it. Caitlin, I am filled with a special gratitude for your sincere interest, support, and committed effort in the design process. However, I am especially grateful to you for sharing your favorite warm shawl, which you so sweetly draped over my shoulders in a wheat field in Oklahoma—a special moment captured that became the cover of this book.

In partnership with our three marketing wonders, I was assisted by Tamara Hurwitz's Production Services team at KWRI. My deepest gratitude goes to Swava Pearl Hooks for the internal layout of the book; Mary Keith Trawick for project management of the layout design; Jeffrey Ryder for his copyediting gift; Owen Gibbs for his careful proofreading; Samantha Garza for sales and customer service in delivering this book to our Keller Williams associates at Family Reunion; and Cory Rose for the setup of the website sales and technology that makes order fulfillment a success. Last, but never least, I have unending gratitude for Tamara. She has been my publishing liaison, advocate for my business success as a writer, and she has navigated my journey during the physical production of this book. I think Tamara may have a little "velvet hammer" in her, since her sweet, smiling disposition is balanced with just the right amount of "tough" to make her a perfect champion.

I cannot thank our Mar/Comm and Production Services staff without acknowledging Jim Talbot, COO, and Danny Thompson, executive director of operations, for their support and love, which under-pinned our KWRI team's availability to serve me on this endeavor. As Mark Willis often says, "everything rises and falls on leadership"—and, gentlemen, I am grateful for yours.

I want to express my deepest gratitude to Dave Jenks for helping me articulate the lessons of this book. He began this work in 2008 when he was serving as vice president of research for KWRI. I told him that many Keller Williams associates were asking me to speak about my life story and personal viewpoint. So, Dave interviewed me for several hours and then transcribed those interviews. He then formed an outline of the important events of my life and Keller Williams leadership, which became the foundation of my "Morning with Mo" presentations and, ultimately, this book. Dave suggested the title "Lessons from a Tenant Farmer's Daughter" because of the significance of early Dust Bowl experiences and the simple but powerful wisdom I learned to apply to my business leadership.

So many times during my tenure as CEO, Dave was my wordsmith. I called him the Aaron to my Moses, referring to the Old Testament Biblical story about Moses leading his Nation while Aaron was the teacher who used his speaking ability to help people understand. Thank you, Dave, for being my wordsmith once again. I hope I have done justice to the words.

I am compelled to offer a special thank-you to Ravi Zacharias for his willingness to write the foreword to this book. Ravi, I am honored and humbled by the beautiful words you scribed for me. You have been so instrumental in deepening my faith and strengthening my Biblical understanding. I have such respect for the worldwide work of your ministry and for the powerful books you have written. Thank you for blessing mine.

Always present at my side with a positive word and shining smile, I offer my sincere and deep appreciation to my loyal executive assistant, Kellie Clark. So much more than an assistant or an administrator, you have been my teammate and partner in so many fun projects—including this book. Thank you for your gift with words, your unending patience, and your long battery life during late hours or weekends spent writing. Thank you for your genuine and heartfelt smiles, squeals of delight, and choked-back tears that punctuated our hours spent reading this book aloud together. We have shared nearly ten productive, creative, wonderful years. I cannot wait to see what we will accomplish in the next decade to come. You are, and will always be, a treasured gemstone that brightly illuminates my world.

My *encouragers* are as important to me as those who physically contributed to the work of writing. From the earliest moments of my executive career as CEO, Althea Osborn has been a sustaining force in my life. Both a dear friend and a trusted colleague, Althea, you have been an inspiration, a sounding board, and a role model. Thank you for your influence in my life.

Sharon Gibbons, we all owe you a debt of gratitude as Gary's first employee and staff member—you have been loyal to this company through thick and thin for more than two decades. Personally, I am grateful that you have been my encourager, friend, and solid supporter from the moment I stepped into the KWRI office as CEO. You stood by me and lifted me up when I had to de-hire staff and leadership in order to get the ship turned around. During a time filled with uncertainty, you helped to navigate with me through rough seas. It is a joyful feeling to stand on the bow of the ship, sailing smoothly and looking to the horizon at our future possibilities. Thank you, Sharon, for your loyal business companionship.

As regional director of the KW Oklahoma region and my longtime friend, Sherry Lewis, your presence in my life has been a ray of sunshine. In good times and in bad, when life is easy and when it's tough, whether we are problem solving or celebrating—you have offered me your gift of kind words, your fun-loving nature, and a reason to feel inspired. Sherry, you keep my bucket full.

Nina Rowan Heller, with positive words of support and your vast knowledge of both mental and physical well-being, your investment in me over many years has contributed greatly to my goal of living past 100 years. Nina, I deeply love and appreciate you.

Linda Paxton, you have the gift of reaching inside my heart to articulate my most deeply held feelings. Our creative collaboration over the years has earned you a very special home in my heart. I appreciate you more than you possibly know.

Monica Reynolds, your friendship, travel partnership, and business collaboration are an invaluable resource for me—a well into which I dip my cup and feel refreshed with every drink.

Ellen Curtis, I thank you for your pragmatic words of wisdom and your support offered very early in the writing process, when my creative ideas were still nebulous and taking form.

Jeremy Conaway, you have been an encourager to our company and its leadership for many years. Foreseeing our direction, you advocated for our business models and culture at a time when we were just beginning to break the bonds of "Keller Who?" in our industry. There are not words to adequately express our appreciation for your longtime support and friendship. You have blessed us.

Along with my encouragers, who have all been a source of light and love, I cannot neglect all of those through whom I have succeeded in business. Without you—whether you are aware or not—I would not have reason to write this book. Beginning with Ruth Honeycutt and Jerry Brown, my first business partners—real estate has been a magical journey. Enthusiastically, *we thought we could and so we did* create great success together! Ruth and Jerry, you will always be the pearls I found in life's oyster.

Some of you have been fixtures in my Keller Williams life from its inception. To John Bridwell and Paul Woolsey, I extend admiration, respect, and sincere thanks for your pioneering spirit and business acumen, through which we succeeded together at a level higher than we ever imagined. I offer my gratitude to my original Core Group partners, whose influence, integrity, and real estate experience were invaluable to the early success of the Oklahoma region: Dennis Nevius, Bob and Jerry Brown, Charles Tritthart, Gary Atchley, and Carlita Walters.

To my precious friend and colleague Gene Lowell— without you, I would have never made the fateful introduction through which Gary Keller *found me.*

Looking back over my life's events—connecting the dots—I sincerely believe that you were God's instrument. Gene, you are the angel He sent to lead me to my destiny at Keller Williams. Thank you for your many years of friendship and business partnership; it is my honor to know you and to love you.

I am compelled to acknowledge all of the KW associates and leaders who have helped to build and grow the Oklahoma region, which I own. I am especially proud of and grateful for the skilled leadership provided by the OK team leaders and owners: Adelina Rotar, Susan Miller, Susan Beach, Sheila Farmer, Elizabeth Raines, Julie Smith, Shelley Koster and Whitney Virden, Casey Cook and Shelan Whitehead, Russell Mulinix and Peggy Wright.

Outstanding in the Oklahoma region are Adelina Rotar and Susan Miller, team leaders in the two market centers that I personally co-own. As OP, I could not work with finer leadership than you. You each demonstrate a high level of accountability and commitment to growth. However, most precious is the loving way that you tend the garden of our KW associates that thrive in your fields. I am so proud of you.

I offer special thanks to Kate Scott and Lisa McClellan, who form the OK regional leadership team with Sherry Lewis—you are invaluable to us all.

Together, associates and leaders alike, you form an amazing team of professionals whom I am honored to be in business with each and every day. I am grateful for your hard work, integrity, and the success that we have created together.

I extend heartfelt thanks to all of our Keller Williams regional leadership. Thank you for trusting us with your business *partnership*. Some of you have remained committed to our company and its executive leadership for the entire duration of my career. Your longevity speaks volumes about your faith in Keller Williams, your belief in our culture, and your love for this company. I would like to offer my special gratitude to Sherry Lewis, Ruth and Herb Taylor, Bruce Hardie, Cheryl Sadoti, Tony Brodie, Ginger Gibson, David Osborn, Scott Agnew, Wendi Harrelson, Carol Cones, Colette Ching, Erica Hill, Paul Morris, Tom Lamphere, Bryan and Marci Fair, Lee Beaver, Mike McCarthy, Todd Butzer, Madison Offenhauser, Joe and Mary Harker, Brenda Benson, Bob Kilinski, Georgia Alpizar, Mark Olesh, Mike Tavener, Mike Brodie, Seth Campbell, Dick Dillingham, Gary and Nikki Ubaldini, Jimmy and Linda McKissack, John Davis, Chris Heller, David and Marian Benton, and Carl Nardone.

To the KWRI staff—you are the finest group of professionals ever gathered under one roof. When I took the role of CEO, I could count the number of our international employees on one hand. Today, our team is blessed with more than 200 talented, loyal, and hardworking stakeholders who serve our KW associates and leaders at the highest level. I am filled to the brim with pride in all of you—occasionally it overflows out of my eyes in the form of joyful tears. Our entire executive team owes you a debt of gratitude, as we succeed through you each and every day. Thank you for making this a company that no one would ever want to leave.

I have limitless appreciation for the professionals who volunteer their service to KW Cares as its board of directors: Mary Tennant, Sharon Gibbons, Brenda Benson, Steve Chader, Jean Grubb, Doris Carlin, Julie Costa, Ben Kinney, Julie Lane, Holly Priestner, Danny Thompson, Diane Mitchell, John Prescott, and Beverly Steiner. With your dedicated and loyal partnership, we have taken an idea born in the Austin Southwest market center and created a multimillion dollar wellspring of service and support for Keller Williams family members with emergency needs. You are the coolest group of people that I have ever known. Additionally, I have unending gratitude for Kathy Neu, executive director of KW Cares, who leads an all-star staff in service of our great cause, daily. Kathy, we simply couldn't do it without you.

To the precious ladies who gather with me to pray for our company twice each month—Kellie Clark, Sharon Gibbons, Adele DeMoro, Mary Harker, Michelle Steele, Nikki Ubaldini, Kay Evans, Linda McKissack, and Doris Carlin—I want to extend my most heartfelt and joyful gratitude for remembering my book-writing endeavor in prayer. As you lifted up prayers to the Lord, my heart was lifted by your faith and love. Each of you is an angel on earth.

To Lisa McClanahan and Jason and Lainee Copeland—without your daily service, support, patience, and effort, my world would cease to go around. You are equally precious and invaluable to me. May each of your lives be blessed, as you have blessed mine.

Betty Shaw, thank you for your creative contribution to every corner of my world—and especially for making Stonemill beautiful, *twice*. You were a source of light, hope, and encouragement when it was dark for a short time.

The most fulfilling and challenging roles in life can be mother and grandmother—especially when counterbalancing these with a career. Rick and Margie, Karin and David, Andee and Alex, Conner and Parker—you have always been my Big Why. Creating an abundant, comfortable, warm, secure world for you has been my driving force every day. I love you more than you will ever know.

To all those who have attended my training, my KW Family Reunion sessions, the Inspirational Breakfasts/Brunches, the Cultural Summits, and all the regional "Morning with Mo" events, I give you my deepest appreciation. You have been there for me, encouraged me, and made me feel special. You have given me the hope and the courage to write this book. It is for you, along with my children and grandchildren, that I have written it. May it provide you with guidance, inspiration, and a joy-filled life.

Finally, to every reader of this book. Thank you for contributing to my *dream come true*. I love you. God loves you. No matter the difficulties you encounter along the way, may you always live with joy in your heart, a song on your lips, and your cup overflowing with abundance.